CELESTIAL
GODDESS
RISING

AWAKEN TO THE CELESTIAL REALMS
AND IGNITE THE SACRED FIRE OF YOUR SOUL

KATY SLOANE

Celestial Goddess Rising: Awaken to the Celestial Realms & Ignite the Sacred Fire of Your Soul

Copyright © Katy Sloane, 2022

First Edition

ISBN (paperback) 978-1-914447-65-5

ISBN (ebook) 978-1-914447-66-2

Book Design by Faye Williamson.

Author Photo by Elizabeth Ellery.

Interior images: Elizabeth Ellery, Samantha McIntyre, Shutterstock.

Prepared for Publication by TGH International Ltd.

www.TGHBooks.com

This book is dedicated to
Gracie and Lennon. My two angels.

I love you.

CONTENTS

INTRODUCTION

Do you ever feel like there is so much more to life than what you perceive with your five senses? Or like sometimes there is someone or something trying to get your attention? How many times do you tell yourself it's 'just my imagination', before going back to dealing with life's daily dramas and mundane chores?

Maybe you see repetitive number sequences like 1111 ... Or maybe you have those spooky déjà-vu moments, when you feel that you have already done something that you have never done or visited somewhere that you have never been.

Perhaps you thought about something happening and then, as if by magic, it happened! We all have those freaky moments when we go to call someone and then out of the blue, before our finger can press dial, they call us. Coincidence? Nope! There is no such thing as coincidence. This is the Universe, and all its synchronistic beauty, trying desperately to wake you up!

Well, I have excellent news for you light warrior ... There is indeed so much more to life than your five senses, and so much more to life than we have been led to believe through our limiting systems and stereotypical views of how we should live our lives.

From the moment of birth, we have been conditioned to fit into a box that looks something like this: go to school, get your qualifications (or not), go to work and pay your taxes, get married, have kids, get sick, die. Sound familiar?

Now, I know this isn't the case for everyone, but this is the 'norm' that has been thrust upon us our whole lives, and if the 'norm' is your life's dream then good for you, no judgement ... but I think it's fair to say that depression is a global epidemic and so many people are living their lives never finding happiness and never even coming close to their true potential. Why? Because we have voluntarily enslaved ourselves into a system that simply does not serve us.

So, I say it is time to break out of the 'norm' and to remember the truth of who we really are, to remove the shackles of social conditioning and to enter into a new way of living, because there is nothing normal about you. You are an extra-ordinary, multi-dimensional being of light and, if you don't believe me now, then you will by the end of this book!

You are about to be taken on a journey where you will open your heart and mind to the higher realms of existence and invite some very powerful celestial beings in to help you, opening your eyes to a new, exciting world of infinite possibilities where abundance flows in every area of your life and happiness is no longer a dream, but your natural state of being.

There is an army of angels and light beings just waiting to assist you on your life's journey, waiting to guide you to meet your true potential and walk your highest path. How do I know this? Really, though, like how do I actually know this?

It is said that when a yogi has a mystical experience, he knows he cannot share it with others because it cannot be understood, it can only be experienced. Well, I'm certainly no yogi, but I have had many mystical experiences. I'm choosing to share them with you, here and now in this book, because I know that even though you may not understand them, it may help you to see that there is so much more to life than the physical realm. I believe that we can all have mystical experiences because we all come from the same Source. We are beings of light in a physical vessel, and when we start realising this truth we can begin to awaken to our multi-dimensional selves.

I am going to share with you some powerful personal truths that I have only ever shared with a handful of people in my life so far. I have kept these experiences mostly to myself for many reasons – the main ones being fear of ridicule, being branded crazy, not being 'cool' (I know, who cares right?) and having my work discredited, but if there's anything the year 2020 has taught me, with all of its chaos and division, it is to break through the barriers of fear (especially fear of judgement) and to step powerfully into my truth. There is so much freedom in shedding the fear of being judged by others. Please know that any form of judgement comes from the ego and it is always a reflection of the way a person feels about themselves; it is a reflection of their level of consciousness and mental state. Remember, it is never about you and always about them.

Only those who are ready to hear this information will truly hear it. Many souls will not be ready to break free, they still have lessons to learn and karma to balance and that's okay. We each have our own unique path. So, now please allow me to share my truth with you in the hope that it may help you to step into your power and share your truth also.

The Great Awakening

The very fact that you are reading this now is a sign from the Universe that you are awakening to the truth of who you really are.

Right now, we are experiencing a mass awakening on the planet. This time has been prophesied for aeons; it is the time when we as a species evolve into the next stage of human consciousness. It is a time when truth is being unearthed after being buried for so long, and through the integration of this truth we become empowered sovereign beings. It is a time when the old paradigms and systems of control crumble and we realise we are all connected ... a New Earth is dawning and this is, indeed, a very exciting time to be alive!

As you read and absorb the information within the pages of this book, know that they are imbued with high vibrations bringing about powerful activations to help accelerate your spiritual growth and guide you to walk your highest path. I have included exercises to help you to integrate the information presented and to heal and release any blocks or trauma you are holding onto. I recommend having a journal handy so you can note any feelings or thoughts that arise during the exercises. I have created a special Celestial Goddess Rising journal, which you can download for free at **katysloane.com/CGR** and I have also recorded the audio to all meditations in this book, so you can simply relax and enjoy them – you're welcome!

Throughout this book I will refer to the Source, the Creator, God, as both He and She because it is about time we brought our skewed perceptions back into balance.

I have split this book into three parts to echo my own journey of awakening:

Part One – Celestial: You will learn about the divine masculine archangels and the importance of calling upon our Celestial friends for help … this was essential in laying the strong foundations for my own spiritual path.

Part Two – Goddess: You will learn about the divine feminine archangels and the Goddess aspect of the Creator that has been suppressed and diminished for thousands of years. As we awaken to the truth and power of the Goddess, we will begin to restore balance, both personally and collectively, and therefore to the entire planet itself.

Part Three – Rising: You will learn about the great shift to 'New Earth' and how to raise your vibration so that you may rise up and break through the illusion of fear. Let this book be your road map to ascension, giving you a broader perspective of the Cosmos and the celestial beings that are collectively cheering us on and helping us as we rise into the golden age of Aquarius and anchor in a New Earth of peace and harmony.

So, now I have some serious questions for you …

- Are you ready to tap into your true power and connect with an army of celestial light beings?

- Are you ready to crack open the chrysalis to which you have been bound for so long and spread your wings and fly?

If the answer to both of these questions is yes, then prepare for a paradigm shift, as you free yourself from the chains of the past that have held you back for too long.

My intention is for this book to unleash the light warrior within you, elevating your vibration, expanding your mind, raising your consciousness and igniting the sacred fire of your soul by connecting to the celestial spheres and the powerful light beings within them. May you light up this Universe and shine bright like the fiery stars from which you are made!

The great awakening is upon us. It is time.

The First Visitation

Let me take you back to 1988 to meet my five-year-old self. At this point in time, I was living in a small semi-detached house on a peninsula called 'Wirral' in North West England. One evening, I was getting ready for bed and after putting my cosy peach terry towelling pyjamas on, I went into classic Katy daydream mode (a state I often found myself in). That day at school there must have been something pretty thought-provoking in religious assembly, as while my mother was taking her time cleaning out the bath, I was sitting on my bed in a trance, singing to myself. Now, this was no ordinary song. I was singing out to God and I was asking a very important question that had been troubling my five-year-old self for quite some time … I can't remember exactly how the melody went, but I know that the main chorus with the all- important question went something like this: 'God if you are reeeeeaaaaal, then why can't I see yooooouuuuu?' I know, catchy right? As my high-pitched voice rang through the ethers, what happened next left me speechless (perhaps that was the point!).

The frequency of my bedroom instantly changed. It was as though someone had flicked a switch into another dimension and a mysterious being of light appeared before me. I was filled with a blissful feeling of pure love, manifesting as a great tingling warmth within me. It was like there was a beautiful golden sun ablaze inside my heart, radiating its fiery, loving light throughout every cell of my body.

I gasped in utter shock, as the awesome apparition manifested in front of me. The being appeared masculine and had long white hair and a long white beard, smoother than silk. He wore a draping garment of white light and his face was so kind, gentle and familiar. His hair appeared white, but it was not physical hair like we know it, and he was certainly not old and wrinkly like you would expect a human to be … No, he was not of this world. Each strand of his hair looked like it had a million tiny rainbows weaving and flowing through it, yet it was white. The light of his garment draped over him like a waterfall, flowing perfectly over his etheric form. To be clear, there was nothing physical about this being; he was made of pure light. With a subtle glint of humour in his eye, he opened his arms out with his palms facing upwards, presenting himself as if to say, 'Well, here I am and, yes, I am absolutely 100 per cent real!'

His visit was fleeting – not long after he appeared, he faded back into the ethers. As he ascended beyond the veil, the frequency of the room returned to normal and I reached out to him. 'Don't go!' I called out, in a desperate attempt to make him stay a little longer. I did not want him to leave.

You see there was nothing scary about this strange man with his long white hair and shimmering robes. He felt like an old friend who filled me with great warmth and nostalgia. He brought a glimpse of remembrance of a place I once knew, a place that was my true home.

In that precious moment, he ignited a part of my soul that over the years to come would be greatly dimmed by the third dimension and all its mind control, fear and material distractions.

I never told anyone about what I had seen that day. Even at such a young age, I knew that I had to keep it to myself. Perhaps that was the wise old yogi in me knowing that this could not be understood. It would be another 25 years before I would begin consciously working with the angelic realms, and open up and discover more about my kind old friend in his shimmering white robes of light … but you will have to be patient. That is a story for another time.

From Catwalks to Crystals

That was the first mystical experience that I remember, at just five years old. I had no idea how important it would be in shaping my understanding of the divine. As the years passed, I rarely thought about my experience. I became deeply embedded in 3D life with school, sports, playing with friends, and all the usual Earthly distractions. If I'm honest, I did not make much effort to consciously connect to the light, but I consistently fuelled my connection to the higher realms through my artwork. I have always created art inspired by angels, fairies and other realms, and now that makes complete sense. It was as though this magical energy was just bursting to get out and the only way it could be expressed was through my hands onto the paper.

As a young child I was always drawing angels and winged beings, and I still do to this day. If you check out my art shop at **katysloane.com/shop**, you will see an array of golden wings, vortexes and swirling portals of light – nothing has changed! As a teenager, I created an angel wing for my GCSE art exam, which scored me an A. For my A-S level art exam, I recreated the illustrator Brian Froud's epic fairy godmother set in an enchanted woods and for my A2 exam, I brought in my love of fashion and created a painting of Naomi Campbell's classic catwalk blunder, where she infamously fell over in 9-inch purple platform shoes, during Vivienne Westwood's 1993 runway show. I only mention this because even that artwork incorporated an infusion of neon pink feathers from her striking feather boa. I do love a feather, which totally adds up given that it's the number one sign angels will send us!

My love of fashion and art drove me on to art college, followed by university, where I achieved a BA with honours in fashion design. I was all set on the fashion track, having shown my collection at London Graduate Fashion week and even made it onto the UK Sky One hit show 'Project Catwalk' as a designer. I won three challenges and made it all the way to the final challenge, only to be kicked off at the last hurdle by my now friend Nick Ede who was one of the celebrity judges. Ah well, you win some you lose some … and I've totally forgiven Nick for his terrible judgement. Ha!

It's funny how the direction of your life can change in an instant. If someone had told me back then that I would be a spiritual teacher coaching clients and celebrities all over the world to connect to their light and live their best life, in the nicest possible way I would have thought they were crazy! But when you are on the right path things align in ways you cannot imagine and as I trained and studied the art of meditation,

Reiki, crystal healing and angel therapy, my eyes were opened to
the magic of life, and I knew these were gifts I must share with others.
So, over the last decade, I have built my dream business, working with
so many amazing souls and witnessing so many miracles through guiding
them to connect to the celestial realms. There is nothing more rewarding
than watching the miracles unfold after calling in the help, and I am so
incredibly grateful that I get to do this for a living.

A Special Soul

So, when did it all change? How did I come to be a celestial crystal queen
of Zen? And how did I come to be here writing this book on a completely
different trajectory to what I could ever have imagined?

The wise ones say that there are certain special souls that will enter your life
at specific times to alter the course of your destiny. This soul came to me in
2010, bringing a whole new dimension to my life, awakening me from the
illusions of the material world and lifting me onto my highest path … this
special soul is my beautiful daughter, my one and only Gracie Bluebelle.

To say motherhood was a shock to the system would be a huge
understatement. In my perpetual state of exhaustion, I could no longer hear
the call of the catwalk. As I drowned in a sea of nappies, my designer dreams
faded into a distant memory. My days were consumed by feeding schedules,
nap times (or lack of), and all those things you need to do in general to keep
a baby alive and kicking … no pressure.

However, this was all part of the divine plan, as it was amongst the beautiful
chaotic symphony of motherhood that I rediscovered my deep connection
to the angelic realms.

A new chapter in my book of life had opened and, as I navigated the challenges and triumphs of being a new mum, I began to remember my profound connection to the angels.

So, let's backtrack a little to when my angelic awakening began … It is August 2009 and I am heading to Cyprus to be bridesmaid for my bestie Nat on her wedding day. Unbeknownst to Nat and the rest of the wedding party, I had just found out I was pregnant with Gracie and arrived at the airport feeling pretty nauseous with morning sickness. I distracted myself by heading to the magazine stand to see what reading material I could get for the plane. Up to this point I had always been a magazine girl. Don't get me wrong, I had attempted to read books in the past but in most cases I found it hard to get beyond the first chapter. Nope, I had resigned myself to the fact that I simply was not a book kind of gal. Magazines were my jam.

As I wandered towards the magazine rack, I found myself intuitively stopping to scan the bookshelf … at this point I had no intention of buying a book at all, so it was strange I was even looking. A title called 'Angels In My Hair' by Lorna Byrne jumped out at me. I curiously took the book from the shelf and began to read the back cover. This was the autobiography of a modern-day mystic who could see and communicate with angels and spirits. I was hooked. For the first time ever, I bypassed the magazines and headed straight to the checkout. I could not wait to start reading this mysterious book.

From the first page onwards, I could not put it down. As I absorbed the wisdom from the supernatural stories and angelic interactions within this magical book, I began to consciously call upon the angels for help every day.

I had begun to awaken to the magic of the angelic realms and the flurry of signs I received in response to my calls were mind-blowing. From this moment on, I threw myself into studying angels and explored all matter of spiritual subjects. I was no longer a Harper's Bazaar magazine gal, but an official bookworm, and as I rapidly built my spiritual library of knowledge I transformed into a metaphysical mama, a spiritual seeker on a quest for wisdom and truth. I had found my new passion, activating an insatiable thirst for knowledge of all things ethereal and I was so excited to learn and discover more.

In March 2010 my beautiful daughter Gracie arrived on the Earth plane and changed my life forever. This was one of the most magical, yet challenging, times of my life. After a traumatic birth and a lengthy recovery, I was physically and mentally exhausted. My life had taken a complete 180. I had gone from being a high-flying fashion designer, graduating from fashion school, showing my collection on the runways at London Graduate Fashion Week and starring on 'Project Runway' to becoming a full-time mother, almost overnight. In the first few years of Gracie's life, I felt like I had completely lost my identity. I wondered if I would ever have any time to do anything for myself again ... for any new mums reading this, hang on in there, it gets easier and I promise that you will feel like your own person again.

When Gracie turned one, I moved to New York City with my husband Barry, who happens to be an actor. He had landed a role in the phenomenal play 'Jerusalem' written by Jez Butterworth. After its amazing success in London's West End, it had been transferred to Broadway. So, off we went as a family of three on an adventure to the Big Apple ... so glamorous, living the dream, right?

Err, well actually it was far from it. I found myself completely isolated in NYC. I was a new mum in a concrete jungle, with no support network at all … and with Barry working crazy hours I was pretty much a single mother with a baby that would not sleep. And when I say that, I mean she WOULD. NOT. SLEEP. Gracie stopped napping at the age of one. When bedtime came, she would scream and scream until she vomited … it was not unusual for me to be up in the night with her between 10 to 15 times … and she wasn't about to grow out of it anytime soon either. At the age of three, she was finally diagnosed with sleep apnoea.

Needless to say, I was really struggling in the Big Apple and I started to call upon my angels night and day, asking them to bring me strength and help me to get through this.

The sleep deprivation and exhaustion started to take its toll on my body and, one particular weekend, I began to feel pretty unwell. It was a Saturday and Barry had two shows that day, so he was gone from 11.30am to almost midnight. This felt like one of the longest days ever. I rapidly declined throughout the day with shivers, fever and, more alarmingly, I had a swelling on my neck that seemed to be gradually travelling up behind my ear towards my skull. I asked my angels for help and I knew I needed medical attention; this was serious. By the time Barry arrived home at midnight, I handed over the baby reins and jumped a cab to the nearest hospital. I have never wanted my own mother more than on that day when I was in the waiting room of a foreign hospital, completely alone. However, I took great comfort in knowing that I wasn't really alone; I knew I had the angels at my side. I could sense them cocooning me in their light and I knew I was going to be okay.

Upon being examined by the doctor, he sent me for an emergency MRI scan. This meant injecting a dye into my bloodstream, which was extremely unpleasant. Okay, that's an understatement – it felt like burning fuel had let rip through my veins and all the time I overrode the trauma by breathing deeply and communicating with my angels. I knew they had my back and I knew that ultimately everything would be okay.

After running multiple tests, I was diagnosed with cellulitis and put on a drip with strong IV antibiotics. After a couple of hours, I began to feel much better. Thank God the antibiotics were kicking in – I had turned a corner and was officially on the mend. I told the doctor that I had to get back for my baby and so he reluctantly discharged me from the hospital at around 5am. As I checked out at reception, I was hit with a medical bill of $8,500 and asked to pay as much of it as I could … welcome to America! Thankfully, I had travel insurance so I paid a couple of hundred dollars and then deferred the bill to the insurance company. Jeez, how I felt for the millions of people who had no health insurance, and how incredibly grateful I am for the free health care I had taken for granted my whole life in the UK!

As I stepped out of the hospital into the pitch-black concrete jungle, there wasn't a taxi in sight. Realising I could be waiting a long time, I began to walk in the direction of my apartment, hoping that I could flag a cab on the way. It was scary to be out walking at that ungodly hour on my own, particularly in my fragile state. As I walked, I prayed I would be home safe soon and called out to the angels for protection. As I did this, a shift occurred and the darkness began to lift as the golden sun started to rise over the Big Apple. Walking in a daydream, it was as though I had entered a meditative state. I felt the fear melting away as it was overridden with pure gratitude.

I thanked God for my health and for the angels that I knew were at my side. In what seemed like no time at all, I found myself stood looking at the lobby to my apartment block, which was around two miles from the hospital – that would be a tiring walk on a good day, let alone after the gruelling 24 hours I had experienced. Yet I had somehow walked all that way without even breaking a sweat. 'Divine intervention' I thought … or maybe I had time-travelled? Anything is possible when the angels are working their magic!

When I look back to that day, there was so much angelic intervention that occurred. The doctors said if I hadn't gone to the hospital that night, I would have most certainly been kept in for several days as the infection was spreading fast. Thankfully the antibiotics zapped it before it got too bad. I am so grateful to the angels for their guidance, protection and for the cocoon of love I felt during that traumatic time. As with all our challenges, lessons are learned and I realised from then on that self-care was essential. I had to look after myself better; I could not let myself get so low and run down again. As mothers, we so often put ourselves last, but we are the glue that holds everything together and without us everything falls. We must start putting ourselves first so that we can be the very best version of ourselves mentally, emotionally and physically for our children and everyone else. They say it takes a village to raise a child; well, I certainly didn't have a village, but I did take it upon myself to get a sitter. Her name was Barbara and she would come in for an evening here and there so I could meet Barry for dinner. Sometimes I would book her for an afternoon so I could explore the city, she was a God send … literally!

As an artist my creativity had been completely stifled since becoming a mum and this was really taking its toll on my mental health.

I decided I needed a creative outlet to stay balanced. Truth be told, I have always loved acting; it lights me up and I find the escapism of playing different roles so therapeutic. After discussing my creative options with my husband Barry, he decided to book me onto an acting class, which conveniently fell on the one night a week he didn't work – it was divinely aligned. On Monday evenings I headed to Judy Henderson's 'acting on camera' class to nurture my inner drama queen and I absolutely loved it. As I walked through Hell's Kitchen, coffee in one hand, script in the other, running my lines, I smiled with gratitude as in that moment I was free. I got to be Katy again and it felt so good. Having this much-needed time for myself was a game-changer and getting to play different roles and honour my creative self was so good for my soul. Through making these positive changes I became a more present and attentive mother, and both Gracie and I began to enjoy and embrace our big adventure in the Big Apple.

My Spiritual Sight

It was while living in New York that I began to see blue sparks of light appear sporadically. These sparks were mostly around Gracie's crib, but also appeared in very random places. For instance, I would be making a cup of tea and a spark would appear at the side of me. I had no idea what this meant and wondered if I was going crazy in my sleep-deprived state!

Six months flew by and we returned to London where I continued to see the sparks of light. At this point my logical mind had kicked in, full force, and I decided to get my eyes tested. Sure enough there was nothing wrong with my eyes – I had 2020 vision – and when quizzing the optician about the blue flashing lights, he looked completely puzzled and had no idea what on earth this could be.

Once again, I decided to go inward and soothe my troubled mind by meditating and asking the angels what was wrong with me … to which I was told a very loud and resounding 'absolutely nothing'! In this meditation I began to see the same colour in my mind's eye – a beautiful blue spark of light igniting within my mind, illuminating my third eye and this was when I realised that what I had been seeing was in fact angelic energy. Wow.

As soon as I finished my meditation, I grabbed my laptop and typed 'seeing blue sparks of light' into the search engine. I knew I couldn't be the first to experience seeing angelic energy in this way. Astonishingly, one of the first things that popped up was 'The blue angel'. I had full body tingles as I read about this fascinating phenomenon of seeing blue lights, which was apparently linked to Buddhas, mystics and the great enlightened masters.

I realised there was nothing to worry about … far from it; an incredible gift had been activated within me. I couldn't believe it – all that time spent thinking I had some neurological problem when in fact my spiritual sight was awakening!

This is a typical example of how our logical minds create a whole lot of unnecessary worry. Wow, so I was actually seeing angelic energy, but even cooler was the discovery that the vivid blue colour was connected to Archangel Michael who works on the blue ray of light. The pieces were falling into place and I couldn't wait to dive deeper into learning more about the unseen realms and how to communicate with our celestial friends.

As your spiritual sight develops, you may also begin to see sparks of light. This is almost like friction from angelic energy around you and is a sign that the angels are with you and letting their presence be known.

As my spiritual sight has developed over the years, I am now able to see all different coloured lights, not just blue. I have learned that each of the colours relate to the different kinds of angels and archangels; it is amazing to be able to see the type of angelic energy around people. It is a spiritual life tool that helps me immensely when working with my clients and I am so grateful for this gift that is constantly growing through my consistent connection to the realms of light.

You too have spiritual gifts; it is just a matter of awakening them.

Opening Your Intuitive Channels

We all have four main channels of communication with the angels:

1. Clairsentience (clear feeling)

2. Clairvoyance (clear seeing)

3. Claircognizance (clear thinking)

4. Clairaudience (clear hearing)

Let's take a look at the kind of signs you should expect to receive over the next few weeks as you dive deep into learning and connecting with the celestial realms. Many of you will have already been receiving lots of these signs, especially as you have been guided to read this book.

To help identify your strongest channel of communication, refer back to this section of the book or use your downloadable journal at **katysloane.com/CGR**

Create a tally of signs you receive within each of the four categories below.

Clairsentience – clear feeling

- Feeling tingles or waves of energy.

- Rustling of the hair/crown chakra.

- Sudden temperature changes.

- Air pressure changes.

- Feeling a blanket of energy around you.

- Feeling a pulling sensation (usually around the solar plexus and crown).

- Sensing a presence.

- Smelling a fragrance, such as flowers, that has no connection to the physical plane.

Clairvoyance – clear seeing

- Seeing repeated number sequences like 1111, 444, 333, 222.

- Seeing sparks of light physically or with the third eye.

- Seeing colours in the third eye (particularly in meditation).

- Receiving mental images or impressions in your third eye.

- Receiving visions in the dream state.

- Seeing orbs.

- Seeing physical signs, such as feathers, coins, butterflies, angel clouds, coloured mist.

Claircognizance – clear thinking

- Having an innate knowing about something which you have no previous knowledge of.

- Spontaneous thoughts guiding you to do something.

- Speaking words of wisdom and not knowing where they came from (a form of channelling).

- Having the feeling that you knew something was going to happen before it happened.

Clairaudience – clear hearing

- Hearing messages through songs.

- Hearing a voice (often this happens as we are waking from the sleep state).

- Hearing high-pitched frequencies or ringing in the ears.

- Hearing unusual sounds (this can be the angels trying to get our attention).

- Receiving a message from a stranger or overhearing a conversation that relates to something you need guidance with.

Remember, it is never a question of if angels are trying to communicate with you, as they are always trying to communicate with you. It is simply a matter of recognising the signs and fine-tuning your intuitive channels through practice and repetition.

Make it your mission to invoke your angels every day and soon enough it will come naturally to you, allowing you to receive their uplifting messages with clarity. The more time you put in to connecting and learning about these powerful celestial beings, the deeper connection you will have with them.

Where focus goes, energy flows.

Seeing Beyond the Veil

So, before we dive into awakening your gifts, let's get into the science behind our spiritual sight. Did you know your physical eyes can only see a slither of the energy that surrounds you? To be precise, only 0.0035 per cent of the electromagnetic light spectrum is visible to the average human eye. Let's just take that in for a moment – it means there is so much more to your reality that you can't see than what you can see with your physical eyes!

Note that I said 'physical eyes' – that's because you have a spiritual eye, known as your 'third eye'. The third eye is an energy point in the centre of your forehead between the brows and it plugs into the pineal gland within the centre of your brain. This tiny pinecone-shaped gland contains rods and cones just like your physical eyes … I know, pretty cool hey?

The ancients knew this and they knew the importance of the spiritual eye. The pineal gland shows up constantly in ancient Egyptian symbology and hieroglyphs. It is even symbolised on the Buddha ... did you know his classic pinecone-shaped head represents the pineal gland? There is ancient symbology all around us holding powerful wisdom just waiting to be unlocked. We just have to open our eyes and start paying attention.

As your third eye opens, your intuition will be greatly enhanced and you will begin to sense the angelic light that is all around you. By the time you reach the end of this book, your third eye will be awakening from its slumber, intuition will be your new superpower and, before you know it, communicating with angels, archangels and celestial beings will be your new 'normal'.

Intuition Ritual: Opening Your Third Eye

Do this quick and simple exercise daily to help open this energy centre.

1. Close your eyes and breathe deeply.

2. Place your awareness in the space between your brows and imagine a white orb of light appearing in the centre of your forehead.

3. Now imagine a white orb of light appearing in the centre of your brain, illuminating the tiny pinecone-shaped pineal gland.

4. With every breath in, see the white lights expand.

5. Breathe deeply and feel these two orbs begin to merge, creating one beautiful orb of white light.

Reiki

Reiki was a major catalyst in my awakening and accelerated my spiritual growth beyond measure. Through learning this healing art, my intuitive channels were cracked wide open and my communication with the higher realms was taken to new levels.

Another very special soul who incarnated on the Earth plane shortly after Gracie in 2011 is my nephew, Stanley, who did the same for my sister as Gracie did for me. He shifted her onto a completely different path and through his journey she awakened to her innate powers of healing … and so did I.

Stanley was born with a bowel defect and had to have major operations from just a week old. It was during this incredibly challenging time that the angels came through in full force and guided my sister and I to learn the practice of Reiki. The magic and miracles that flowed and continue to flow from our journey with Reiki are unbelievable. I talk more about Stanley's story and healing journey in the Celestial section of this book under Archangel Raphael, the angel of healing.

Lots of people ask me what Reiki is. In short, it is a hands-on healing system that brings balance and harmony on an emotional, physical, mental and spiritual level. It harnesses the universal life force or ki energy that flows through all living things. This can also be referred to as prana.

There are many techniques that stimulate the flow of prana around the body, such as acupuncture, Qi Gong and yoga, to name but a few. However, what I love about Reiki is that it is so easy to learn and practise, and absolutely anyone can do it, regardless of their religion or beliefs. The techniques are super-simple to master and the results are profound.

Learning Reiki is a powerful way to raise your vibration and an excellent way to lift blocks and shift unwanted energy from your aura and physical body. There is so much more to Reiki than just healing ailments; it supports all aspects of your being and balances the non-physical energy around you, known as your auric field. It is so important to keep your aura strong and balanced, as this is where all dis-ease begins. When energy blocks are not lifted, they gradually become denser and denser, eventually manifesting as dis-ease within the body. Reiki is therefore a great preventative therapy as it sweeps away those blocks before the unwanted energy manifests within the physical body.

There are three traditional levels of Reiki, with a fourth level designated for teacher training. I believe each level unlocks a deeper awareness and understanding of energy and the higher dimensions.

I have had many miraculous experiences with this healing art form and it has enriched my life in ways I could not have imagined possible. When I first learned Reiki, I had absolutely no intention to practise it professionally. However, the universe had other plans in store for me and as soon as I had completed my level 2 training, clients began to come to me out of nowhere.

They would be sent to me through word of mouth and every time something amazing happened. It was so exciting knowing that each session was unique and provided so much expansion for myself and for the client.

In the beginning, I would offer energy exchanges with friends. For instance, my friend Lilly is an amazing make-up artist and she loves all things ethereal like me. So, I would give her Reiki and in exchange she would paint my face for an event. There was always a glamorous Hollywood party to attend with my husband, so it was the perfect exchange.

We had some amazing Reiki sessions. During one of them, I felt the warm, loving energy of Lilly's dad, who had passed away a year previously. I also kept receiving an unusual impression in my mind's eye of a little bridge with water underneath. The bridge was very specific and had triangular structures across it. I often receive images for clients during Reiki and, even though these may make absolutely no sense to me at the time, I know I must share what I have seen as it could be an important message. At the end of the session, I told Lilly I felt her dad was checking in on her and I did a rough sketch of the image I had seen. As she looked at the sketch, she took a step back and gasped in utter shock. I asked her what was wrong and she said, 'Oh my God it's my dad, it's my dad! I have to show you something!' She grabbed her phone from her bag and scoured her camera roll before showing me a photograph of an almost identical image! There was a little bridge with triangular structures and flowing water beneath it; this was her dad's favourite place to visit and they had not long scattered his ashes at this very location on the bridge! As tears of joy rolled down her cheeks, she thanked me over and over as she knew that her dad was letting her know that he was just fine. Reiki had brought her so much comfort in knowing that her dad was very much alive and guiding her from his non-physical perspective.

That is why there is nothing quite like Reiki, because you never know what a session will bring and there are so many layers to healing. It's not just about the physical. As word spread, my services were in high demand and, before I knew it, I was fully booked with a waitlist. I think the Universe was definitely trying to tell me something.

I have been practising Reiki since 2011 and have never once had to advertise my services; the angels just kept on sending me souls in need of this deep healing and angelic connection … they were telling me that this was an important part of my path. I have now stepped into a new chapter of my Reiki journey as I teach my own certification programme to students all over the world. There is nothing more rewarding than empowering my students to heal themselves and others.

The cool thing about Reiki is its versatility – you can apply it to all areas of your life. The energy can be used to create higher outcomes within certain situations and it is an excellent tool for accelerating manifestation … and oh how I love the magic of manifestation!

I will never forget doing a Reiki session with a client called Kira. After discussing what areas of her life needed more balance, Kira expressed she would like to focus on manifesting more work opportunities and abundance. This was to be our intention for the session and we, of course, asked her angels and team of light to oversee everything for the greatest good. We called on Archangel Ariel (archangel of abundance) and Archangel Chamuel (an archangel that guides us in our career) to help align magical opportunities for Kira. As I began to give Reiki, I could feel the energy clearing away Kira's mental and emotional blocks and bringing her into a state of flow.

At several points in the session, I had a vision of her running up a wall … so random, I know. The vision was zoomed in on Kira's feet, she was wearing sneakers and actually running up a vertical wall. This was definitely an odd one to interpret and I figured it must be some kind of metaphor, perhaps a message for her to realise she is so much more powerful than she knows and that the laws of gravity don't apply to her? Ha! I was confused about the message, but even so I knew I must tell her.

At the end of the session, we discussed the things that we had both felt and I gave her some exercises to support her in manifesting great things into her life. As she was about to leave, I could hear my angels urging me, 'Tell her, tell her', so I stopped resisting and decided to fully commit, as crazy as it sounded: 'Kira, one more thing … err, I did have a couple of visions of you running up a wall.' Okay, she officially thinks I'm mad …

'Oh,' she replied, with a confused stare. 'Really? That's cool … What does it mean?'

'To be honest, I'm not sure. It might be a metaphor. I'm pretty sure all will be revealed further down the line,' I assured her.

She left feeling uplifted and excited for the divine opportunities flowing to her.

A few months went by before I received a video message from Kira. The message alongside the video read: "OMG YOU SAW IT!!! HOW COOL IS THIS???!!" I opened the video excited for the big reveal and couldn't believe my eyes … There was Kira defying gravity and running up an actual wall!

She had booked an amazing job with Nike and the advert she was shooting required her to run up a wall in Nike sneakers! Not only was this an amazing career opportunity that had manifested through Kira investing time for herself to heal, release and connect to the higher realms through Reiki, but it was also a profound message for me to continue to speak my truth no matter how insane it may sound at the time!

Reiki has played a huge role in my own awakening, giving me a deeper connection with the angelic realms and the Cosmos as a whole.

Chakras

Did you know you have powerful energy centres, called 'chakras', within your body that distribute the flow of ki or prana? I had no idea what chakras were until I began my Reiki training in 2011. It is now second nature to work with them and I wonder how I ever didn't know about them. If there is an imbalance in my body, I can instantly relate it to a particular chakra. For example, if I'm having headaches I know my crown chakra needs balancing, or if I'm feeling angry then my throat chakra needs attention. The chakras are an essential aspect of understanding the subtle energy fields and the complex energy pathways active in our body.

Here is a little summary of what chakras are:

Chakra means 'spinning wheel' in Sanskrit and that is exactly what they are – spinning wheels of energy. We have seven main chakras within the physical body and each chakra is responsible for supplying energy to specific parts.

Our chakras work on many subtle levels and can be affected by our emotions and the external vibrations we are exposed to. When they become blocked or imbalanced, the body is more susceptible to disease and the flow of energy is diluted. Each chakra has its own colour and vibratory rate, starting from the base of the spine up to the top of the head.

The seven main chakras and their locations are:

 The crown chakra (purple or white): Top of the head.

 The third eye chakra (indigo): Between the brows.

 The throat chakra (blue): Throat.

 The heart chakra (green): Centre of the chest.

 The solar plexus chakra (yellow): Upper abdomen.

 The sacral chakra (orange): Just below the naval.

 The root chakra (red): Base of the spine.

As we make the shift into higher states of consciousness, other chakras outside of the physical body within the auric field will become active. These are known as the advanced chakras, but that is a chapter for another book.

There are so many layers to your being that you cannot see, and I'm not just talking about your chakras; you have a huge aura surrounding your physical body that contains many subtle layers of energy. You are so much more than a physical being, and as you tune into your spinning wheels of light you will begin to align with the energy of your divine self. You are a powerful light being within a physical vessel and your potential is unlimited.

Your aura is an energy field which stretches way beyond your physical form – this is scientific fact. The first layer of your aura is known as the 'vital body', this is the densest layer and the easiest to see. It follows the contours of the physical body perfectly and usually radiates around 4 to 6 inches outwards.

The second layer of your aura is known as the 'astral body' but I like to call this your 'emotional aura' as it is constantly changing with your emotions. It can display an array of colours reflecting your mood. Much like your chakras, if you are happy and in good health your aura will be bright, vibrant and expanded. If you are depressed, fatigued or in a state of dis-ease, your aura will be small and dulled with more muddied colours coming through. The third layer is called the 'mental aura' and is shaped like an egg enveloping the physical body, vital body and astral body. This layer is much more stable than the emotional aura and acts as a barrier to external lower vibrations. It is a protective layer that can be strengthened with focused intention. For this reason the mental aura can be more highly developed in some people than in others.

Most of us cannot see auras because the frequency of light is out of range for the average human eye.

However, there are many clairvoyants that can see auras and I am grateful to have been able to see some myself on rare occasions over the years.

Thankfully anyone can now see their aura through Kirlian photography, which can capture the colours of your energy field. One of my lovely Reiki students, Angelina, is the founder of 'Soulglow' aura photography in California and I am grateful to have seen and experienced her beautiful aura photography first hand. In August 2019, I booked a family aura portrait session for myself, my husband and the children. At this time, my daughter Gracie had just started fourth grade and had moved to a new school, which was really tough for her. She was unhappy and stressed and this was reflected in her aura picture, which showed up as a dull red colour.

Barry was working away in Memphis and could only come home every other weekend; it was tough and he too was unhappy. Interestingly his aura was almost identical to Gracie's – both were small, displaying the same dull red colour.

Fast forward eight months later and thankfully we were all in a much better place. My husband had come home after finishing his job in Memphis and my daughter had moved to a new school where she was flourishing and happy. As the holidays approached, I began preparing for my annual 'holistic holiday boutique', something I put on for my clients and friends at my home in Los Angeles. This was always lots of fun as guests got to mooch over an array of sparkly crystals and holistic goodies, with a hot chocolate or mulled wine in hand. This particular year I invited Angelina to come and offer her aura photography services at the event. However, she was heavily pregnant and the event was just past her due date, so Angelina gave me a tutorial on how to use the camera, just incase she couldn't be there on the day. On the morning of my event Angelina gave birth to a beautiful baby girl called Sienna! It was time to put on my multi-tasking hat and become the aura photographer for the afternoon. I was so excited to experiment and see what kind of colours would show up in everyone's aura.

I decided to re-take Gracie and Barry's aura pictures to see how different they looked eight months on, and I am so glad I did as the difference was astounding! Both of their auras were so much more expanded and vibrant in comparison to the photos taken eight months earlier and this was a perfect reflection of their emotional state. It was fascinating to see this beautiful change, but what was even more fascinating was how similar our auras were. Mine and Barry's were almost identical and carried the same vivid orange colour with a fiery halo of magenta light around the outer edge and Gracie and Lennon's held the same colours too – incredible!

This was so validating as I had been teaching my students how to protect their energy field for years. I would always tell them, 'Be careful who you spend your time with; the energy of those around you will directly impact your energy.' And now I had physical evidence to show this. Barry and Gracie's aura photos completely supported this notion. I can confidently say that our aura attunes to the energy that is around it … just let that sink in a minute.

'Your aura attunes to the energies that are around you.'

So, the people you spend most of your time with will either uplift or deplete your energy. Don't panic – there are ways to shield your energy field to protect you from being drained by others, but for now take a moment to assess the energy of those that you spend most of your time with.

Energy Analysis

Take a piece of paper and list five people who you spend most of your time with. Now ask yourself whether these people uplift your energy or deplete it. Put a tick for those who uplift and put a cross for those who deplete. Now review the list. If most of them deplete you, then it's time to shake things up a little and spend more time with those people who make you feel good. Now I know with family members and colleagues this can be difficult. I have a lot of clients that are constantly drained by their family and co-workers, yet inevitably have to spend a lot of time with them. If you can't keep the energy vampires at bay, then you can do a simple shielding technique every day to help strengthen your aura, making it less susceptible to depletion from low-vibe people.

Remember we all have times when we are low vibe, it's part of being human. Show compassion to these people as they are likely going through a tough time and hold this low vibration because they are unhappy.

Energy Ritual

Visualise yourself in an egg of white light and say this affirmation:

'I am divinely protected from all lower vibrations.
My aura is strong and uplifts those around me.'

Positive affirmations like this one are powerful statements that will expand your aura, uplift your energy and strengthen your protection. Meditation is another practice that will give your aura a powerful boost. In her book, 'The Power of Auras,' author Susan Shumsky writes: 'Practising meditation is the most profound way to increase the vibrational frequency in your auric field and thereby transform your life.' And I wholeheartedly agree.

Note: I talk about shielding your energy field in more depth in the 'Celestial' section of this book under Archangel Michael. If you are an eager beaver and want to do this exercise right away, feel free to skip to page 61 but don't forget to come back!

Meditation

I'm a sucker for a meditation. There is nothing more effective at lifting and shifting your vibe than getting in the zone and letting the stress and tension melt away. But it wasn't always this way, I was once a complete bobblehead (a phrase adopted from Shaman Durek in his book 'Spirit Hacking' that refers to being fast asleep) and I had no idea where to even start with meditation. I like a good laugh and meditation just seemed a bit too serious and woo woo for me … cut to the present day and I'm a meditation teacher conducting classes around the globe. I'm all in with the woo woo and I freaking love it!

The first time I was asked to practise meditation was in my Reiki level one training back in 2011, which my sister and I did together. Our Reiki master sent us into the back room of her house to sit cross-legged on the carpet in front of some pretty impressive mirrored wardrobes. My sister had been out on the town the night before (not recommended the night before Reiki training, but then she's always been a rebel) and she had fallen over and hurt her coccyx. So, rather than having to sit cross-legged, she was designated a special chair in the middle of the room. She stuck out like a sore thumb and I couldn't help but find it all rather amusing. 'Be serious,' I berated myself inwardly 'and whatever you do, do not laugh.' Oh God I could feel the corners of my mouth trembling with amusement, which did not bode well as we hadn't even begun the meditation yet.

Our Reiki master Jane entered the room. 'Be serious,' I thought. 'We will do 15 minutes of meditation and then it will be time for a light lunch,' she announced.

Just to clarify, my sister and I had literally never meditated before ... like ever. 'Just close your eyes and focus on your breath,' she continued. 'Okay, I can do that,' I thought.

'Just don't think about Sarah on that chair, whatever you do don't think about her.' It's important to mention that my sister and I are always laughing at each other ... not in a mean way, but just because we are generally funny people. Sometimes she need only glance at me and I will crack up laughing, so I desperately needed to focus my attention on my breathing and not on her.

About five minutes into the meditation all was going well, until I heard the slight creak of a door followed by some clicking noises. I curiously squinted my eyes to see where the noise was coming from. That was when I saw our Reiki master stood in the doorway taking photos of the class, the rest of whom were in deep meditation. As I directed my glance towards the mirrored wardrobe, I saw my sister sat on her special chair, arms crossed over her chest, head tilted back ... she was so in the zone that the corners of her mouth actually protruded downwards towards her chin forming a full-on trout pout. Well, that was it, I was gone. I could not contain myself as I let out the most inappropriate laugh, disrupting the whole meditation class. Epic fail.

To make things worse my startled sister opened her eyes to see what I was laughing at and soon realised it was her. This then sent us both into a spiral of uncontrollable laughter. It was so bad that we had to leave the room, taking refuge in the bathroom next door. We were laughing so hard that no actual sound was coming out of our mouths and the hilarious thing was my sister still didn't know what I was laughing at!

For at least ten minutes we laughed silently in the bathroom as she tried
o fathom what on earth was so funny and it was only when I pointed to
her face and then mimicked her trout pout that she got the joke!

This birthed one of our favourite expressions – 'medoface' – our scouse
hybrid abbreviation for 'meditation face'.

We still laugh about it to this day and relive the memory of the whole
hilarious saga. Whenever either of us is upset, or triggered by something,
we will tell each other to 'go and get your medoface on'. It never fails to lift
the vibe.

Thankfully our Reiki master saw the funny side that day, although she did
advise we be separated until the laughter subsided, so I was sent to finish
my meditation on the stairs … the naughty step, I thought! Ha!

I love telling my students and clients to laugh as much as possible and to
not take everything so seriously. I feel like there is so much seriousness
around spirituality and it can really take the fun out of the journey. I love
to lighten the mood and show that it doesn't have to be so serious; there
is so much joy to be found in the little moments and we are here on Earth
to have fun!

I love to bring an element of humour into my classes. Laughter is so high-
vibe and healing … hence the expression 'laughter is the best medicine'.
In her book 'The Secret,' Rhonda Byrne tells an amazing story of a woman
who healed herself entirely of cancer through laughing; she literally
watched sitcoms every day!

Anyway I digress – back to meditation. So, after the epic fail in my first ever meditation class, I decided to make up for it by throwing myself into this amazing practice and learning as much as I possibly could on the subject. I experimented with every form of meditation I could find and, after a few weeks, I was officially hooked. You see meditation is a bit like going to the gym or to an exercise class; it's a workout for the mind and you've got to find the style that you love. Once you do, you'll never look back!

My favourite kind is, of course, guided angelic meditations! There is nothing more uplifting than taking time for yourself by journeying into the realms of light through meditation. It's pure bliss and is without a doubt the most powerful way to connect to the celestial realms. As you explore the meditations presented in this book, you will receive many signs from our celestial helpers.

SUMMARY

- Humanity is experiencing a shift in consciousness and you are part of it ... how awesome is that?!

- Angels are real and want to help you. You have free will, so invite them in.

- You have a third eye with rods and cones in the centre of your brain called the pineal gland, which can help you to see energy that you can't see with your physical eyes.

- You have four main ways of communicating with your angels and guides: Clairsentience – clear feeling; Clairvoyance – clear seeing; Claircognizance – clear thinking; Clairaudience – clear hearing.

- Reiki is a catalyst for awakening.

- Your body is so much more than you have been led to believe. You have seven major energy centres, called chakras, that run from the base of your spine to your crown.

- You have an energy field that extends out past your physical body, called your aura. The condition of your aura reflects your mental, emotional and physical state.

- Your aura attunes to the energy around you. Spend time with those that uplift you.

- Meditation is your superpower. It will create a greater connection to the celestial realms and transform your life.

PART ONE
CELESTIAL

PART ONE:

CELESTIAL

So, let's dive deeper and learn more about our celestial friends …
on that note, what does the word celestial even mean? Let's take
a look at the dictionary definition:

Ce.les.tial

Adjective

- Positioned in or relating to the sky, or outer space as observed
  in astronomy

- Belonging or relating to heaven

- Supremely good

The first definition is the scientific explanation of 'celestial' and refers
to coordinates of star systems and constellations etc. It is a common
observation of the third dimensional universe from a logical human
perspective. It's okay to be logical, but if we want to create some celestial
magic in our lives then we're going to have to dig deeper and bat logic
out across the Big Dipper!

Most of us think of celestial beings as other worldly and completely separate from us mortal humans here on Earth, but celestial energies simply exist on a different frequency to ours. This frequency is, in fact, all around us; we simply have to tune in to it to feel the uplifting, healing vibration of our angelic friends.

The second definition: 'Belonging or relating to heaven'. When thinking of heavenly beings, most of us will play a montage in our heads of angelic winged-like beings flying around on puffy, white clouds playing a harp or a golden trumpet. Or maybe you have a vision of cupid floating along with his bow and arrow, surrounded by a flurry of red beating hearts. OK, it's time to smash that old record right now and shine a new light on this.

Maybe you believe in heaven, maybe you don't – either is fine – but what if we think of heaven as a state of being? A state of pure high-vibrational energy that is free from the stresses and strains of our physical third-dimensional reality here on Earth. If we think of heaven in this way, then this definition is pretty accurate, because celestials do vibrate on a much higher frequency than us human beings and therefore they are closely related to that high-vibrational state of bliss that many of us call heaven. The truth is we are all related to and belong to 'heaven'. We have all come from that state of pure high-vibrational light from the Creator; this is the very essence of our soul. We just got a little muddied down here at 'Earth school' and that's okay. The mud is what builds our character, makes us stronger and evolves our consciousness on many levels. By wading through the mud, we can accelerate our journey further into the light.

The third definition 'Supremely good' is pretty accurate. Celestial light beings are indeed 'supremely good' and they are here to help and guide us to live our best life. So, let's shake off any fears of the unknown or any misconceptions that you may have and embrace the opportunity to work with these divine helpers. Prepare for life to get a lot more magical. Celestials bring it on – we are ready for you!

CHAPTER 1

YOUR CELESTIAL TEAM OF LIGHT

Everyone has a celestial team of light, whether they believe it or not. This is a group of energies that were assigned to your soul from birth to guide you. Within this team there are many different beings, including angels, ancestral guides, ascended masters and star guides; these beings will step in at certain points of your life to uplift you and steer you in the right direction.

So, let's look at the different kinds of energies you will likely have in your celestial team …

Angels: there are many different types of angels that will help you in your Earthly life, such as teacher angels, archangels and guardian angels, to name but a few. Everyone, without exception, has at least one guardian angel.

Ancestral guides: these are souls within your family lineage that have taken on the task of being a guide for you in your physical incarnation. They are assigned to you from birth and have usually passed over to the spirit world before you were born. They take on the role of guide to aid your growth, but also their own growth. It is a two-way street; you are always learning from your guides, but your guides are also learning from you.

Ascended masters: these are enlightened souls that have incarnated as human beings and have balanced and transcended karma. They often leave behind their own unique legacy of light, having made great waves in helping humanity and raising the collective consciousness and vibration of the planet. Jesus and Buddha are two well-known examples of ascended masters. Dr Usui, the founder of Reiki, is also an ascended master, leaving behind his legacy of the universal energy healing system that is Reiki. Other ascended masters include Mother Mary, Mary Magdalene, Quan Yin, St. Germain and, last but not least, Melchizedek. There may be certain ascended masters that you are connected to on a soul level, who may oversee certain points of your soul's mission. If an ascended master is part of your team, it is a great honour and you most likely have a powerful spiritual mission in your Earthly life.

Star guides: these guides are from other highly evolved planetary spheres and star systems, and are connected to your soul in some way, most likely because you have lived past lives within their planet or sphere of existence. This is a tough one for many to comprehend, but I want you to think of the infinite nature of your soul which has lived in many different forms and existed in many different places throughout the multiverse. The only reason you may doubt this is because you passed through the veil of amnesia to be here on Earth and pretty much forgot everything; that's the great challenge of the Earth plane and that's why it is known as the hardest place to incarnate in the Universe. Part of your mission is to remember your divinity, to remember where you come from and to begin to lift that veil of amnesia.

Your star guides will help you to remember the multi-dimensional nature of your soul and discover your cosmic connections.

So, now we have clarified who your celestial team of light are, I think it's safe to say there is an abundance of celestial energy all around you, just waiting to assist you on your life's path. All you need to do is ask for help and invite them in. You see, when we decided to incarnate here at 'Earth school' and plummet through the veil of amnesia into the realm of separation, we were given free will. Our angels and guides will not usually override this free will, so it is very important that we invite them in. This is super-easy to do and, honestly, you don't need a fancy ceremony to call in your team of light. However, I always recommend creating a sacred space in your home to remind you to connect with them.

Creating Your Sacred Space

Your sacred space could be as simple as having a candle and a crystal on your bedside table or, if you love to go all out, you can really get creative and add flowers, feathers, essential oils and anything that makes you feel good. Make it your new habit to wake up and stand or sit in front of this sacred space, centring yourself before taking a breath and inviting in your celestial team of light.

Here is a simple invocation to help you do this:

> *'I call upon my celestial team to be with me now. I am
> ready to expand my awareness and connect to my angels
> and guides. Please guide me and surround me with light.
> Thank you.'*

You have just sent out a powerful invitation to your angels and guides. Boom, it's that simple … let the magic and miracles flow!

Signs and Synchronicities

Now that you have called upon these powerful light beings and invited them into your life, you will start to receive an abundance of signs from your celestial friends. Keep your eyes and ears open and make a note in your journal of any divine synchronicities and signs you notice – see illustration below for some of the most common ones.

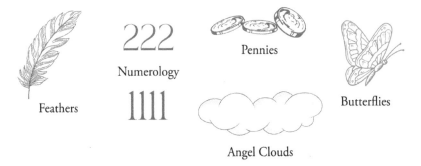

Feathers

222
Numerology
1111

Pennies

Angel Clouds

Butterflies

The angels are divine messengers and mediators between Earth and the higher realms. There are many different kinds of angels present throughout all of creation, but I particularly want to talk about the archangels as they have played such a huge role in my own spiritual journey and awakening. I cannot wait to share with you my own personal experiences with these incredible light warriors.

The Archangels

There are an infinite number of archangels and each has a particular role to play within the multiverse. Each one has been assigned its own divine mission and comes with a unique skill set. In this book I have included the archangels that I work with closely, covering the areas of life in which we seek balance … love, health, career, relationships etc.

The archangels have been spoken and written about for aeons; they are mentioned across many of the holy scriptures such as the Bible, Torah and The Quran. However, I want to stress that angels are not religious; they are incredibly powerful universal energies that are for everyone, no matter what your religious or spiritual beliefs.

A lot of people tell me they don't like to call upon angels because they feel they are taking them away from helping others. Don't worry, the archangels are unlimited beings, meaning that they work on all planes simultaneously and are not limited to one location at a time, like we are in our dense, physical bodies.

The archangels can be with anyone, anywhere at anytime, simultaneously all at once, so you are absolutely never taking an archangel away from anyone. I know, pretty mind-blowing hey?

I am passionate about sharing my truth and my own unique experiences with the archangels so that you may feel empowered and inspired to connect with them too. Through this powerful connection to our celestial friends, you can begin to walk your highest path and live your best life.

Another fun fact about the archangels is that they each work with different coloured rays of light. We can visualise specific colours to connect to specific archangels. You may begin to see the colours spontaneously appear as sparks of light in your third eye chakra, or perhaps even with your physical eyes.

Masculine and Feminine Energies

I am excited to present the archangels to you as a perfect balance of divine masculine and feminine energies. Every archangel has a masculine aspect and a feminine aspect; the feminine is sometimes referred to as the archeia'. It is important to remember that everything is vibration and, in truth, angels are genderless beings of light, but to our human minds it is easier for us to perceive them as masculine or feminine. This is why there is no right or wrong when it comes to identifying the archangels as being masculine or feminine, because it really comes down to our personal perception of them and we all perceive things differently.

The key to our awakening and ascension – to enlightenment – is unifying the masculine and feminine energies within us.

For thousands of years, the masculine energy has dominated this planet, diminishing and oppressing the sacred feminine. This has kept us trapped in lower states of consciousness and, as a whole, we have forgotten our own divinity.

Activating and balancing your brain activity is an important part of tuning into the higher frequencies of your celestial friends. Your brain is the vibrational centre of your body, with two very complex hemispheres. Most of us are ruled by the left hemisphere, which is the analytical centre of logical, linear thinking. This represents the masculine energy. The right brain is the creative, intuitive centre that is directly connected to your higher self. This represents the feminine energy. When we unify the left and the right hemispheres (the masculine and feminine), we begin to awaken to our true potential, realising the souls multi-dimensional nature as the higher self is united with the physical self.

Imagine the things we will be able to do when our brain is balanced and unified; it is a vital part of our awakening and conscious evolution. Meditation is a key player in this process as science has proven that meditation awakens parts of the brain that are usually inactive. As you charge up your main vibrational centre through spiritual practices like meditation, prepare to unleash your superpowers!

To help you, I have paired a quick and easy guided meditation with each archangel, which you can access for free on my website **katysloane.com/CGR**. Enjoy!

The Divine Masculine Archangels

Allow me to introduce you to four powerful Archangels that I work with closely in my own life and healing, as well as in mentoring sessions with my clients. These are Raphael, Michael, Uriel and Zadkiel. I perceive these powerful celestial beings to emanate a divine masculine vibration but, as I said earlier, angels are genderless so this is simply my interpretation. I am excited to share with you the amazing direct experiences I've had with these incredible light warriors over the years.

Each archangel carries its own frequency of light, which manifests as colour. One of my favourite ways to connect to specific archangels is through visualising their colour. You will find the colour for each one, as well as their main qualities, beneath each heading.

Here is a colour guide for the divine masculine archangels:

Michael   Raphael

Zadkiel   Uriel

CHAPTER 2

MICHAEL

Strength, protection, releasing fears.

Colour: Electric blue

Probably the most well-known of all the archangels, Michael is the great protector, and is incredibly powerful, bringing strength and helping us to tap into our personal power. This angelic warrior carries a sword of light and helps us to release fears that are holding us back, empowering us to speak our truth and follow our divine life purpose. If you need any form of energetic or physical protection, look no further, Michael is your guy.

Michael also aids us in releasing fears on a global level, helping to lift the vibration of the planet and the collective consciousness. I think it's fair to say he's been a pretty busy guy these last few years, with the tsunami of fear that came with global lockdowns, numerous viral variants (scaryiants) and the political chaos that unfolded in 2020.

The craziness of this unprecedented time had me calling upon Michael pretty much every day, and not so much to dissipate my own fear, but certainly to help shift the collective fear.

I want you to imagine the collective consciousness as a complex grid of energy that surrounds the planet. We are each connected to this grid and, almost like an electrical outlet, we are plugged into its energy. Each individual adds their energy to the whole and are connected to each other via this intricate grid.

Simply put, our energy always falls into one of two categories: love or fear. If we are in fear, we upload fear to the collective consciousness, so if there are billions of humans in a state of fear that's a seriously dark cloud of energy being cast across the entire planet and, unfortunately, this will only create more things to be fearful of. We are powerful creators; we create our reality through our thoughts and emotions both on an individual and a collective level.

Einstein knew this, Buddha knew this, Jesus knew this, all the great masters knew this and, unfortunately, the handful of people at the top of the pyramid pulling the strings also know this. We are programmed to be in a constant state of fear through the media, news and television. Fear creates dis-ease, dis-ease creates sickness, sickness creates a lot of money.

The good news is we can switch out of mass fear consciousness pretty quickly and, thankfully, those of us who are aligned and connected to the light are far more powerful on an energetic level than those who are not, so we can quickly override the lower vibrations of the collective.

That is why change starts from within. Before you try to help heal the world, align yourself in the vibration of love. It is the most powerful thing you can do to help the Earth and humanity.

My gorgeous client and star sister AnnaLynne McCord has created an amazing movement called 'The Love Storm,' which aims to end human trafficking and modern-day slavery from the inside out, by organising mass meditations around the globe and harnessing the light into the collective mind. Check it out at **thelovestorm.com**

Mass meditation is an incredibly powerful way to send waves of light into the collective and there have been some amazing experiments performed that prove its power. I talk more about this in the Rising section of this book (see page 262).

If you ever feel like you are being sucked into collective fear energy, or if you are in a situation where you feel afraid or vulnerable, then Michael is the archangel to call upon. You can invoke his presence with this simple invocation:

> *'Archangel Michael, please be with me and surround me with your powerful electric blue light.'*

Michael works on the blue ray of light and is connected to the element of fire. Whenever I see the blue within the centre of a flame, I instantly think of Michael as this is the colour of his energy.

Michael first started appearing to me back in 2010 when I gave birth to my daughter, Gracie, and he has continued to show up for me ever since.

His electric blue light manifests around me on a daily basis, as I consistently call upon him for strength and protection.

Blue Flame activation

This is a powerful technique I use, and teach to my clients, to connect with Michael.

Find a quiet space and light a candle. Stare into the flame of the candle for a minute, focusing on the blue light within the centre.

Breathe in deeply and say this invocation:

> *'Archangel Michael, please be with me. I wish to connect to your protective and strengthening blue light. Thank you.'*

You may feel the vibration of the room change when you do this, or perhaps see a flash of blue light in your third eye.

Shield Your Field

One of my most popular techniques with Michael is to invoke his shield of protection. We can ask Michael to shield us from negativity so that only the highest vibrations of love and light may come through to us. Here is a quick and easy visualisation and invocation to help you do this:

Take a moment to close your eyes and go inward. Take a deep breath and say this invocation:

'Archangel Michael, please surround me with your shield of light. May only vibrations of love and light enter through this shield. I am divinely protected.'

Now visualise a protective blue shield of light all around the outer edges of your aura.

Give thanks to Archangel Michael.

Boom … your shield is up and you are good to go!

I always love to give this invocation to my Reiki students and clients as it is so simple yet so powerful. The affirmation 'I am divinely protected' really empowers the invocation as it affirms that it is already done. I will talk more about the power of affirmations and your divine 'I am' presence in the 'Rising' section of this book (see page 236).

This practice is excellent for doctors, nurses, healers, therapists and anyone who works closely with people in a state of dis-ease.

Energetic Cord Cutting with Michael

Michael is often depicted with a sword emanating blue flames of light. His sword holds great symbolism and is an alchemical sign of purification and releasing fears.

One of the most powerful practices we can do with Archangel Michael is energetic cord cutting. We are constantly creating energetic connections with people and through some of these connections, especially romantic ones, we create energy cords. Every interaction, thought, emotion and feeling is added to the cord, so if there is a lot of disharmony within a relationship you can imagine how heavy that cord will get.

Sometimes when we leave one relationship and enter into another, we repeat the same patterns because we are holding onto that disharmonious energy and carrying it forward.

The good news is that energetic cord cutting helps to release these negative patterns, so that we can enter and sustain healthy, happy relationships in the future. It is important to note that when releasing energy cords, we only ever release fear-based cords. All cords of love remain and therefore this practice can make a current relationship stronger. That is why it is particularly effective to continue regular cord cuttings, even in present relationships.

I have performed many cord cuttings on my clients over the years and the results are truly amazing. Aside from most clients being able to physically feel the energy being released from the body, it is the symbolic interactions and undeniable signs that follow afterwards that leave them astounded.

One of my clients, Jane, came to me after a long and painful divorce. She was an actress and her husband felt he could not support her career, which led to arguments, resentment and deep animosity between the couple. Jane was most upset by the fact that amongst all the fighting, she had lost her best friend. Losing the connection of friendship with her now ex-husband had hit her hard. They hadn't spoken in months.

I suggested we start by performing a cord cutting with Archangel Michael.

She agreed, although she seemed a little unsure of how this would work. I explained a little about the practice of cord cutting and how it can strengthen a relationship with someone by cutting away all of the lower-vibration emotions, which can become anchored into the chakras. I encouraged her to have an open mind and to know that it would be very healing for her.

We set our intention for the session: to release the negative energy cords from her ex-husband. My client fell into a deep, relaxed state and I began to channel Reiki and work with her energy. It felt like pulling overgrown weeds that were crowding her heart chakra; their burrowing dark roots had anchored and intertwined deep down into her solar plexus chakra (positioned over the stomach just above the navel … oh, and this particular client had also been suffering with stomach issues!). At the end of the session, she awoke feeling emotional from the release and felt noticeably lighter; it was 'like a weight had lifted' she said.

As she left my Reiki studio with deep gratitude she burrowed into her bag, pulling out her phone and keys. She looked at her phone and stepped back leaning against the wall with a gasp. 'Are you okay?' I asked. She looked at me with tears welling up in her eyes. 'It's him! I can't believe it! He hasn't contacted me for over six months. He says he is sorry and that he will always love me and support me from afar and that I will always have a friend in him.' She was officially floored (thank God for the wall behind her).

I smiled and gave her a big hug before she left with tears of happiness.

Not only had she got her old friend back, but she had felt the awesome power of Michael and had forged a relationship for life with this mighty archangel. What a gift! I closed the door, took a deep breath and, smiling from ear to ear, I held up my hands in praise and said, 'Thank you, Archangel Michael!'

Cord cutting is beneficial for friends and relatives, as well as for romantic relationships. You know the friend that you go to see, who leaves you feeling completely drained, even several hours or days later? It is because there is an energy cord connecting you to them. People unknowingly drain us of our energy because of their disconnection to Source. I call these people energy vampires … in the nicest possible way! Once you have identified these people, cut the cord and keep them at arm's length. You can send them love from afar or, if you have to see them, then remember to invoke Michael for protection and shield your field!

Remember, your energy field is extremely sensitive and is constantly changing with your emotions and attuning to the energy that is around you. So, if you don't surround yourself with positive people you are going to soak up other people's low vibes … and nobody needs that. Thankfully shielding will help to prevent lowering your vibe and taking on other people's negativity. Phew!

Cord cutting is also particularly good for grief. People are often reluctant to cut cords from loved ones who have passed as they fear it may sever their connection to them, but actually the opposite is true. When we cut cords from our loved ones who have passed, we strengthen our relationship with them in the spirit realm, clearing ourselves of grief and fear of the unknown, and allowing us to hear messages from spirit more clearly.

Most of us will intuitively know how strong a cord is with someone. A good way to measure this is by how often you think about someone, especially if the thoughts are obsessive, manipulative or fearful. Removing cords of negativity also allows us to remove stubborn energy blockages from the past. This process can assist in healing physical, mental or emotional problems and is also excellent for releasing addictions.

Meditation: Cord Cutting with Michael

I have created a special meditation, so you can put this powerful ritual into practice. Find a quiet, comfortable space and allow Michael and his angels to work their magic.

Think of any specific relationships that you would like to release negativity from. Usually, these people will pop up in your mind's eye before or during the cord cutting. It is important to set your intention to release all that no longer serves you from past and present relationships. Remember, you can release cords of grief too. This is incredibly healing for both you and the person that has transitioned.

- Get comfortable and focus on your breath.

- Set your intention to release any cords of fear by thinking of the person or people that you would like to release from.

- Let go of any worries; just be present in this moment right now.

- Bring your attention to your third eye and visualise a beautiful blue orb of light drawing towards you.

- This orb now enters into your space and a great warrior archangel appears before you holding a sword of light. This is Archangel Michael.

- Continue to breathe deeply and with every out breath release the cords, as Michael slices through the energy of fear with his sword of power.

- Many beautiful white orbs of light descend into your space, lifting away the severed energy cords and dissipating fear into pure white light.

- Michael infuses your chakras with his strengthening light and illuminates his great shield all around you. Feel his great protective light enveloping you.

- Start to bring your awareness back to your body. Grounding your energy into the physical.

- Bring your attention to your feet and begin to wiggle your toes. Now become aware of your hands and begin to move your fingers.

- Give thanks to Michael and his legions of light for this powerful energy healing.

Listen to this meditation at **katysloane.com/CGR**

A Blue Ray Visitation

Let me take you back to my 28-year-old self. It was 2012 and I was living in a two-bedroom condo with my husband and two-year-old daughter, Gracie, overlooking the beautiful Ocean Ave in Santa Monica, California.

It is not uncommon for me to see strange things in the middle of the night, but when we lived in this particular apartment I had my angel altar on the bedroom wall at the foot of the bed and I would often send distance healings from here. This was my sacred space, where I would light a candle and tune into the angelic realms. Whilst living in this apartment, I was regularly woken up in the night and would see strange energetic shapes and objects hovering above me. They would stay for several seconds and then disappear up through the centre of the ceiling. I would often give my husband a little nudge to wake him up, before pointing towards the strange object, but usually by the time he had awoken from his slumber it would have disappeared. Most of the time he had no idea what I was talking about and would tell me to go back to sleep. For a while I accepted that these peculiar visions were perhaps just for me; it was most likely my brain lifting in and out of different states of consciousness, but at the same time I intuitively knew I was receiving esoteric information.

There was one particular time when I had been doing some intense ancestral energy healing and I sensed a dark energy that had been lingering around me. I knew this was connected to a troubled soul that had passed and was trapped on the astral plane. The astral plane is almost like an in-between realm that some souls can find themselves in if they have unfinished business or have forgotten their connection to the light.

I was being called upon to help release and heal some of the dark energy connected to that soul, but I was reluctant to get involved.

I am normally a very upbeat person, with a real zest for life, but I'd noticed I was feeling exhausted and pretty low vibe. My higher self knew it was because this energy was around me, but every time that thought popped into my head, my logical mind would tell me 'Don't be silly, the angels are protecting you' and I would distract myself, thinking the feeling would alleviate soon.

I woke up one morning and began to make breakfast for my daughter. I picked up the cereal box and poured some cornflakes into Gracie's bowl. As I tipped the box, I felt a cold thud land on the top of my bare foot. When I looked down, I jumped as on my foot was a large, black scarab beetle. Chills ran down my spine. I knew this was a physical sign sent from spirit and I could not ignore this any longer.

This energy had to be dealt with. I went to my bedroom, lit my candles and said a prayer calling in all my angels and guides for protection. I firmly told the energy to go to the light and asked that the angels help the energy to move on.

That night I went to sleep with my husband next to me and I woke at around 1am to see a spikey mass of black tangled energy at my bedside. I wasn't scared of it, but it wasn't pleasant either, so I instantly called upon Archangel Michael:

'Archangel Michael, please be with me, please protect me and please take this energy to the light.'

As I turned onto my back, I saw a great sphere of electric blue light enter through the bedroom wall. I gasped and quickly awoke my husband, giving him a little jab to the side. As he turned over and looked at me startled, I pointed to the sphere as it flew around the room and over to my side of the bed, consuming the dark energy. The sphere of blue light then ascended up through the centre of the ceiling … just like all the other things I would see. I looked at my husband and he looked back at me in disbelief. 'What was that?!' he said.

'I called upon Archangel Michael to help me and the blue light came into the room. It was Michael!' I said in awe and amazement.

I learned many lessons from this experience, as did my husband. From that day forwards he hasn't doubted my strange visions in the night and I have not doubted my intuition when sensing energies.

I realised that through meditating and sending Reiki and healings from my bedroom I had created a vortex of energy, which had opened a portal, and this was why I would see so many different energies in the night. I am so grateful to Michael for coming to my aid that night and even more grateful that my husband got to see the whole thing too! I am no longer his crazy, hallucinating, sleep-talking wife … well, maybe just a little!

ARCHANGEL MICHAEL SUMMARY

Archangel of strength, protection, releasing fears.

PRACTICES: Energetic cord cutting, releasing fears on a personal and global level, energy shielding, protection

COLOUR: Electric blue

CHAKRA: Throat

CRYSTALS: Lapis lazuli, Clear quartz, Selenite

Breathe, Release, Connect

This striking four piece is inspired by the strength, power and beauty of Archangel Michael and the angelic realms. As you look at this piece may it guide you to connect with Michael and his legions of light. Remember, you can call upon the angels for assistance at any time.

In the center of this artwork is a sacred geometric form called 'the Flower of Life'. This is the ancient and sacred symbol of creation, showing the interconnectedness of all that is.

For more information head to **katysloane.com/shop**

CHAPTER 3

RAPHAEL

Healing, loving relationships, heart activation.

Colour: Emerald green

Archangel Raphael is known as the archangel of healing, aiding us with any health concerns whether it be on a physical, mental or emotional level. He is associated with the green ray of light and works deeply with the heart chakra, assisting healers, doctors and nurses on the Earth plane so that they can do the best job possible with their patients. If ever you are going to the doctors or perhaps a loved one is undergoing surgery, you can call upon Raphael to help the medical team to do a stellar job.

As well as helping us to heal physically, Raphael helps us to heal on a mental and emotional level. It is second nature for me to call upon Archangel Raphael whenever I am conducting a Reiki session and, whenever I do this, he always appears to me in my third eye as a flash of green light. Sometimes I will see his green light with my physical eyes too. Often, if someone needs deep healing, I will see a green light flash around them and, on rare occasions, I will see their entire aura.

As a Reiki healer, Raphael has assisted me many times in client sessions and in my personal life. He is a powerful guide that not only heals us directly with his emerald green light, but helps us to awaken to our own innate healing gifts. I have learned that sometimes we have to be shaken in order to awaken. Let me share with you a pivotal moment in my life when Raphael intervened, helping me to awaken to the healer within and shift me onto a higher life path.

Awakening the Healer

I will never forget the day, 12 December 2011, when I received a gut-wrenching phone call from my sister, Sarah, saying my newborn nephew needed lifesaving surgery. 'Send prayers,' she said. Just five days after her son, Stanley, was born my sister received the devastating news that he had a rare bowel defect and needed to be operated on immediately. He would also need several major operations in the first year of his life.

As soon as she hung up the phone, I went into deep prayer and called upon Archangel Raphael to help Stanley and to help the doctors and nurses do the best job they could when operating on him. However, I had an overwhelming feeling that there was something more to be done; it was as if the angels were nudging me to dig deeper. In times like this it is natural to feel completely helpless, but I was being told that there was another way to help Stanley other than just sending prayers. I listened to my intuition and searched the internet looking for anything that could possibly help Stanley to heal. I found myself Googling 'spiritual healing'.

Initially I had hoped there would be a powerful spiritual healer that I could call upon to go and heal Stanley, like maybe there was an enlightened yogi on tour in the North West of England who could just pop into the hospital and work his metaphysical magic. I've always been a dreamer and was often told I 'live with my head in the clouds', but I just knew that there was something bigger at play here, something that surpassed the physical.

My 'spiritual healing' search on Google directed me to the practice and healing art of Reiki. I had no idea what this 'Reiki' was, but it sounded pretty powerful and if I had understood it correctly, I didn't have to call upon an enlightened yogi to do it or even become one myself. Thankfully, I could bypass the spiritual pilgrimages and simply learn how to channel this healing energy by taking a short and simple course! Literally anyone could do this – wow, I thought, what have I got to lose?

I made it my mission to enrol on a Reiki course. Of course, this had already been divinely aligned because, as if by magic, that very weekend there happened to be a Reiki course taking place just a mile from where my sister and I lived, and as if that wasn't serendipitous enough, the Reiki Master teaching the course happened to be the mother of an old friend of mine!

With no time to waste, I quickly messaged my sister: 'I'm booking on to a Reiki energy healing course to help Stanley. Let me know if you would like to join too.' Initially, I thought she's going to think I've lost my mind, but to my surprise she replied back immediately: 'Yes. Is there space?'

And that right there was the start of a beautiful journey. Both my sister and I embarked on our Reiki level one course and received our training and attunement that weekend.

After each of Stanley's operations, we gave him Reiki healing at the hospital. I will never forget when his monitors were going off as his vitals were out of the normal range. Instantly my sister began channelling Reiki and, as the nurses rushed over, they witnessed my sister giving Stanley hands-on healing. His vitals rapidly returned to normal and the monitor alarms stopped. The nurses were astounded – what a gift! The results and impact of Reiki were beyond what we could have imagined and Stanley was released from hospital early every time, recovering from each of his operations super-quick. We knew that Reiki was the catalyst.

I am so grateful to Archangel Raphael for guiding us to pursue Reiki. He divinely orchestrated events so that we could empower ourselves and awaken to the healer within. We felt his presence and healing light shining over us all during this traumatic time and received many uplifting angelic signs. I will never forget on the day of Stanley's first operation, after calling upon Archangel Raphael and the angels to be with him and oversee the operation, the nurse came to reassure my sister that Stanley had been successfully sedated and the doctors had commenced the operation at 11.11! Wow, in that moment we knew that Stanley was being watched over by Raphael and the angels and all would be well.

Numerology is one of the most common ways that the angels will communicate with us, I have included a summary of angel numbers and their meanings on page 274.

My sister and I are now Reiki Masters and we are so grateful to Stanley for taking on the brave mission to come into this world and awaken us through his healing journey.

Out of the darkest times comes great light.

Archangel of Love

Raphael is also known as the Archangel of love. You can call upon him to help you create harmonious, loving relationships in your life. All you have to do is set the intention to connect with him and ask him for help.

I have to share a pretty cool story with you … In 2012 my husband and I got married in secret in Las Vegas. As I peered into the empty chapel, I saw Barry waiting patiently for me to walk up the aisle to join him. As I looked at him, the most beautiful cocoon of green light appeared all around him. His aura literally illuminated before my eyes with the energy of pure love! I will never forget that day for many reasons, but the most moving vision was seeing my husband completely surrounded by this amazing emerald green light. We were both so present and completely in the moment that day as we said 'I do', with the only witness being the lady that worked at the chapel and the registrar who read us our vows.

The summer of 2013 would play host to our 'real' wedding in a castle in the Cotswolds, England, attended by all our family and friends. Unbeknownst to them, we had already tied the knot, but that was a secret that would be revealed in the evening along with a fun casino, paying homage to our Vegas wedding and bringing a little bit of Sin City Vegas to South West England! However, the overarching theme for our wedding was … you guessed it … angels! We had everything, from feathery floral arrangements to angelic candlelit tables, with each one named after a specific archangel. And did I mention we got married at Cupid's Wedding Chapel in Las Vegas? The chapel that featured in 'The Hangover' with Bradley Cooper, one of our favourite movies. We had so much fun!

Something I should mention is that angels are high-vibe beings and definitely have a sense of humour. They want us to enjoy ourselves, have fun and not take life so seriously! We are here at Earth school to learn, grow and evolve and the best part of that is having fun and truly enjoying our short time here on Earth. We must get out, see new places, try new things, open ourselves up to the abundance of opportunities that are all around us, and create loving connections with our fellow humans. Connecting with the angelic realms will help us to stay motivated and make the most of our time here on Earth.

Raphael will help you to open your heart and embrace life, manifesting loving and meaningful relationships along the way.

Meditation: Heart Healing and Manifesting Loving Relationships

Raphael resonates deeply with the heart chakra and can help us with any issues relating to this, including emotional trauma from relationships and healing from heartbreak. Through calling in Raphael to help us heal our hearts, we can open ourselves up to loving relationships in the future. Raphael will help you to gracefully and fearlessly move forwards with acceptance, compassion and understanding.

Here is a simple visualisation exercise to help heal the heart:

Take a moment to close your eyes and go inward. Take a nice deep breath and say this invocation:

'Archangel Raphael, please be with me
and fill my heart with your emerald green light.
Help me to heal and open my heart so that I
may attract loving relationships in my life.'

- Continue to breathe deeply and visualise a beautiful, green light all around you.

- Breathe in this light and send it into your chest as healing flows into your heart filling your entire heart chakra.

- Now see this light begin to swirl, creating a beautiful vortex of shimmering light.

- This vortex burrows deep into the heart, releasing all the pain and sorrow from the past as it swirls with the healing vibrations of Archangel Raphael.

- Raphael now appears before you, holding his magical staff of healing light. The staff has a caduceus with ornate golden wings at the top and is capped with a magical, emerald green crystal.

- Raphael takes the crystal from the top of the staff and places it directly into your heart.

- You feel great warmth radiating into your heart, as the crystal melts into liquid light, sinking deep into the healing vortex of your heart.

- You take a deep breath and a feeling of great peace and serenity washes over you.

- Raphael places his hand over your heart, sealing this healing light into your heart chakra.

- Feeling gratitude, give thanks before saying aloud: 'Archangel Raphael, thank you for healing and opening my heart, I am ready to manifest loving and harmonious relationships into my life. Thank you.'

Listen to this meditation at **katysloane.com/CGR**

Don't forget to make notes in your journal about any messages, thoughts or feelings that came through in your meditation.

ARCHANGEL RAPHAEL SUMMARY

Archangel of healing.

PRACTICES: Heart activation, all forms of healing, manifesting loving relationships

COLOUR: Emerald green

CHAKRA: Heart

CRYSTAL: Emerald, Green Aventurine, Jade

CHAPTER 4

ZADKIEL

Violet flame, transmuting lower energies, crown chakra balancing.

Colour: Violet

Archangel Zadkiel works with the violet ray of light and helps us to clear the mind of clutter, bringing clarity of thought and helping us to stay focused. For this reason, he is particularly good at supporting students with their studies. If ever you have a lot of work to get through or a test or examination to learn for, Zadkiel is your guy. I will often call upon Archangel Zadkiel when reading books, particularly complex metaphysical ones that require a lot of brain power!

His violet energy resonates powerfully with the crown chakra helping us to retain information; he can even help with memory issues caused by conditions such as Alzheimer's and other forms of dementia.

Zadkiel helps us to clear and balance the crown chakra by clearing away repetitive negative thought patterns.

Often when we constantly worry about something or obsess over a situation or an argument, this energy of worry and fear will anchor in the aura around the head. It is important to release this energy and clear the way for new positive thought forms.

Energy Ritual

Take a moment to close your eyes and go inward. Take a nice deep breath and say this invocation:

> *'Archangel Zadkiel, please clear away the energy and thought patterns that do not serve me. Take any thought forms of worry away and infuse my crown chakra with your violet flame of transmutation. Thank you.'*

As you say this, visualise breathing in violet light and filling your crown entirely with this energy. You can extend this energy practice by sending the violet light all the way down to your toes, filling your entire body with violet light.

The Violet Flame

My story with Archangel Zadkiel began back in 2014 when I was living in Vancouver with my husband and my then four-year-old daughter, Gracie. I had been researching all kinds of magical and metaphysical subjects, as I often do, and had come across Archangel Zadkiel and 'The Violet Flame'.

Something really resonated with me about this, so I decided to dive deeper. In doing so, I found a peculiar little chant that went like this:

'I am the violet fire, I am the purity God desires.'

Supposedly if we chant this mantra over and over we invoke the violet flame of healing and transmutation, bringing a powerful boost to our energy field. 'What have I got to lose?' I thought.

That morning I walked my daughter to preschool through the beautiful landscape of Stanley Park. After dropping her off, I ventured back through the park and began my violet flame chant. I chanted over and over, eventually turning it into an odd melodic tune. I even timed the chant to my walking pace, which over time turned into a weird march, perfectly synchronised with my musical violet flame one liner. Thinking back now I must have looked insane, marching around the park chanting to myself like that!

I chanted my way back to the apartment to embark upon my obligatory mum chores, which I chanted my way through. It actually made doing them a little more fun. Before I knew it, it was time to pick Gracie up from school. I chanted my way back past the beautiful gardens and through the lost lagoon of Stanley Park to get her.

After picking up Gracie, I randomly decided to take her for some afternoon tea. As we walked along the bustling high street, a smell of lavender filled the air and drew me in like a magnet to my dream store called Sage. We quickly detoured into the shop and mooched over the array of holistic goodies.

After much deliberation, I decided to buy a diffuser with lavender oil for the apartment. As we waited in line, I saw the shop assistant staring at me. She seemed somewhat distracted and I had one of those moments where I wondered if I had something silly on my head. Only earlier that week, I had realised I had a pair of sunglasses on my head when I was actually wearing sunglasses, so anything was possible! When I got to the front of the line, all became clear.

'Hello' she said, 'Did you find everything okay?'

'Yes, great thank you.' I replied not really wanting to engage in conversation too much as Gracie was swinging from my arm asking for cake.

The shop assistant hesitated a little before saying, 'I'm sorry, I really don't normally do this, but I just have to ask … Do you know that your aura is the most beautiful colour of violet?!'

My jaw dropped. I was speechless!

I just couldn't believe the words that had come out of her mouth. I'm pretty sure she thought my flabbergasted, jaw-dropping reaction was a little dramatic, but at this point she didn't know the history of my obsessive perpetual violet flame chant that very day!

'You are not going to believe this,' I said. 'I have just discovered Archangel Zadkiel and the violet flame of transmutation and I have been doing a violet flame chant for most of the day, like an absolute crazy woman! Haha!' I was understandably hyped about the whole situation.

The shop assistant was amazed and also relieved that I didn't think she was crazy! She said she very nearly didn't tell me, but her angels would not let it go and kept on at her until she told me … no wonder she was so distracted!

I left the shop feeling utterly amazed and elated. I had never in my then 30 years of life been told by anyone the colour of my aura, ever. And on this day, when I had been doing my quirky violet flame chant march, a random girl decides to tell me that my aura is bright violet. Now that right there is no coincidence … of course not … there are no coincidences!

From this moment on I knew that Archangel Zadkiel and the violet flame were extremely powerful and I carried them forwards into my healing practice and daily life. Since then, there have been many profound healing sessions with my clients and the violet flame. It transmutes, protects, uplifts and heals on an extremely deep and esoteric level, even assisting with ancestral healing over many generations. I am so thankful that Archangel Zadkiel brought this to me so I could share it with you.

Another time when Zadkiel came through very strongly with the violet flame was during a Reiki distance healing session. One of my lovely clients, Arlene, wanted me to send healing to her elderly mother whilst she was visiting her in Chicago. Arlene's mother, Aurea, had been suffering with ill health and her condition had rapidly deteriorated over several months; her spirits were low and she felt very tired all the time. She had never had a Reiki treatment before and wasn't sure what to expect, but as a Catholic she loved angels. We connected on Zoom and I told her that we would be inviting the angels in to help during the session and all she needed to do was relax and receive.

I initially called upon Michael and Raphael for strength and healing, but violet light flooded my third eye and I knew that Archangel Zadkiel was coming through very strongly for Aurea. I began to chant the violet flame mantra and saw all the energy and heaviness that Aurea had carried for so long being transmuted into pure light. I asked Zadkiel to help clear her mind and increase her connection to Source through opening and balancing her crown chakra. The session was powerful!

Once I had sealed the healing and grounded myself, I reconnected to Arlene and Aurea via Zoom to relay my notes and what I had felt in our session. I was not prepared for what Arlene and Aurea would say next …

Arlene explained that as Aurea lay back to receive the Reiki, she started to feel the energy strongly at her crown and around ten minutes into the session she unexpectedly sat up telling Arlene that her mind felt like it was 'expanding'. There were lots of memories from the distant past flooding into the forefront of her mind and Aurea began to talk to Arlene about her childhood. She told her about a lot of the traumas that she had been through, things that she had never shared with anyone before. She also spoke of happy times that she hadn't been able to remember for a very long time, saying it felt as though 'a door had been unlocked within her memory'. She seemed like a completely different person to the one I had spoken to before the session, as she recounted her experience with joy and amazement.

I checked in on Aurea through Arlene for several months after the session and after being in a state of rapid decline, she was now going from strength to strength. Reconnecting Aurea to the light of the angels, and healing and balancing her mind with Archangel Zadkiel and the violet flame, had given her a new lease of life.

What an incredible experience it was to facilitate this session and bear witness to the miracles that unfolded. Thank you, Zadkiel!

Healing the Ancestral Bloodline

Archangel Zadkiel and the violet flame transmutes, protects and heals on an extremely deep soul level, helping to balance karma and heal the ancestral bloodline. He can guide us to connect with our ancestors and heal unforgiveness and past traumas. Sometimes the trauma may not directly relate to us personally, but it remains within the bloodline. By working with our ancestors, we can start to transform patterns of pain and abuse and, over time, regain the vibrant spirit of the family lineage.

Often addictions such as alcoholism will run in a family from generation to generation. If we view everything as energy, then we can see how this energetic pattern of addiction can be held within the bloodline and if it isn't healed by the present generation, it will often be passed onto the next.

Through healing ourselves and setting the intention to heal the energy of our ancestors from the past, we break the cycle and free ourselves and future generations from the perpetual torment of these low-vibrational energy patterns. By breaking the chain, we do a great service not only to ourselves and to our ancestors, but to the collective consciousness of the Earth and humanity. As above, so below.

Dr Daniel Foor, author of 'Ancestral Medicine: Rituals for Personal and Family Healing,' says, 'When we reconcile with ancestors who experienced different types of persecution or who enacted violence and oppression, we make repairs in our personal psyches and family histories that, in turn, mend cracks in the larger spirit of humanity.'

On a collective level, Archangel Zadkiel can help us to heal and transmute historical trauma in relation to race, gender, wars and other types of collective pain.

Interestingly, there was a landmark study in 2013 that showed the transgenerational transference of trauma through epigenetics and gene expression. A team of researchers in Jerusalem showed that children, grandchildren and further descendants of holocaust survivors are especially prone to depression, anxiety and nightmares. These behaviours are tied to a biological marker in their chromosomes that is absent in those not descended from holocaust survivors.

Science is beginning to understand that everything is energy and the pain of our ancestors can often carry through to future generations in order to be healed.

Archangel Zadkiel often works in unison with Archangel Michael and Archangel Raphael. When practicing deep ancestral healing, I always like to call upon all three of them. The energy of Zadkiel, Michael and Raphael together makes an incredibly powerful combo as they work in unison to cut karmic ties, heal and transmute the energy of transgenerational trauma.

Energy Analysis

Identify any ancestral blockages within your family bloodline and think about what side of the family they originate from. Are they maternal or paternal blockages? They could be due to alcoholism, abuse, the past trauma of relatives or your own traumas.

Write down your thoughts and intuitive feelings around this. When you think of your mother's side, how do you feel? When you think of your father's side, how do you feel? Our emotions and intuitive feelings around each side of the bloodline are a strong indicator of what needs to be healed.

Remember you can download your free journal at **katysloane.com/CGR** to guide you with this exercise.

If you do not have knowledge of your family bloodline, tune in to your heart and ask your team of light to guide you in bringing knowledge about your bloodline. Trust what comes through and write down your feelings.

You can also do this practice for adoptive parents and, instead of healing the bloodline, you can heal karmic ties and behavioural patterns.

If you are not aware of any blockages within your family, do not worry. Archangel Zadkiel will transmute and heal trauma even if it is unknown to you at this present moment.

Meditation: Connecting with Ancestors to Heal Past Trauma

Get comfortable and close your eyes. Take a nice deep breath and say this invocation:

> *'Archangel Zadkiel, please be with me. Please guide me as I connect to my ancestors to heal the trauma of the past. Allow your violet light to flow through my ancestral bloodline breaking negative cycles, elevating myself, my ancestors and future generations to come. Thank you.'*

- As you take a deep breath in, visualise a magnificent orb of violet light coming towards you.

- As Archangel Zadkiel and his violet light enters and stands behind you, he illuminates a magnificent shield of violet fiery light all around your aura.

- Visualise breathing in this violet light and sending it into your heart chakra.

- With every breath in, you send this light into the heart chakra, relaxing deeper and expanding this energy centre.

- Now Archangel Zadkiel activates a sacred portal within your heart, connecting to your ancestors.

- He stands before you and places an amethyst crystal filled with violet fire directly over your heart.

- Feeling the light of this crystal radiate into your heart centre, you now see a beautiful doorway of light appear within the portal of your heart.

- You step through this doorway and into a tunnel of pure violet light.

- As you peacefully walk down this tunnel of light, with Zadkiel at your side, you see another doorway. Behind this doorway are your parents.

- As you open the door you see your parents standing before you in a peaceful garden, with flowers, trees and soft golden rays from the sun streaming through. As you stand before them, you feel gratitude for the many lessons they have taught you. Through both good and bad experiences, we are always learning.

- Now Archangel Zadkiel surrounds you and your parents with the violet flame of transmutation and you see all karmic ties and negative energy patterns burn up and dissipate into the light; healing and forgiveness is activated.

- You give thanks and leave this garden as another doorway of light appears and you enter back into the violet tunnel of light.

- As you peacefully move further along this tunnel, you are faced with another door. Behind this door are your grandparents. You can choose if they are on your mother's side or your father's side.

- You enter through this doorway and into another peaceful garden, as you stand before them.

- Archangel Zadkiel surrounds you and your grandparents with the violet flame of transmutation and you see all karmic ties and negative energy patterns burn up and dissipate into the light; healing and forgiveness is activated.

- You give thanks for the healing and leave this room as a doorway appears, leading you back into the violet tunnel of light.

- As you move peacefully through this tunnel, you see that you are now standing at the mouth of a shimmering amethyst crystal cave.

- You enter the cave and see a beautiful crystal chair awaiting you. It is surrounded by many beautiful orbs of light – these are your ancestral guides. They have been waiting for you.

- As you sit on this chair of crystal light, you feel the presence of your guides surrounding you, enveloping you in their soft white light.

- Stay here and rest for a while as you feel their loving support and absorb their divine messages. Pay attention to any thoughts that may come through, and any colours or impressions that flow to your mind's eye.

- As you sit on your crystal chair of light, Zadkiel places another amethyst crystal filled with violet fire over your heart chakra. This crystal creates a bridge connecting back to the portal of your heart and your physical body.

- As you breathe deeply into your heart chakra, your consciousness drifts over this bridge of light and you see the doorway to the portal of your heart.

- Stepping back through the doorway of light, you are united with your physical self.

- Feel the violet light of Zadkiel illuminating every cell of your body, as you ground back into the physical and consciously begin to wiggle your fingers and toes.

- Now taking a moment of gratitude, give thanks to Archangel Zadkiel for the powerful healing you have received for yourself, your ancestors and for the future generations to come.

Listen to this meditation at **katysloane.com/CGR**

ARCHANGEL ZADKIEL SUMMARY

Archangel of violet flame, transmuting lower energies, crown chakra balancing.

PRACTICES: Transformation with the violet fire, enhancing memory, healing the ancestral bloodline, violet flame chanting.

COLOUR: Violet

CHAKRA: Crown and Third Eye

CRYSTAL: Amethyst, Purple Fluorite

CHAPTER 5

URIEL

Wisdom, lifting the veils of illusion, truth.

Colour: Red, gold

Archangel Uriel is known as the archangel of wisdom. He helps us to broaden our perspective and to see the truth in a situation.

Uriel works on the red ray of light and often appears to me physically as sparks of golden, reddish light that is reminiscent of a flame. His name translates to 'Fire of God'.

Uriel helps us to ground in the wisdom of our higher self so that we may move forwards, aligning with our higher purpose. He is often associated with lightning and electricity as he sends us divine flashes of inspiration and motivates us on our journey through life. If you are feeling fatigued, unmotivated or uninspired, call upon Archangel Uriel to light you up from the inside out. He will send a powerful bolt of light to jump-start you into action!

Uriel can also help us by enhancing our discernment and allowing us to break free from the constraints of social conditioning and indoctrination into corrupt systems of control. He will help you to access your true power and self-sovereignty through reigniting your inner wisdom.

Lifting the Veils of Illusion

Archangel Uriel is known as the wisest of the archangels. He helps to activate the truth within us and the remembrance of our own divinity, and the great light from which we came. Through this activation comes a higher awareness and a deeper connection to our higher self and the oneness of the Universe.

As we have entered into the new Golden Age of Aquarius and 'The Great Awakening' is upon us, Uriel is playing a key role in guiding us in our ascension process. We are beginning to purge on levels that we have never experienced before, as we free ourselves from the density of the third dimension, allowing us to move into higher levels of consciousness. When this happens, we will begin to consciously communicate with our angels, guides and the realms of spirit.

As the new age dawns, souls are preparing to navigate through the veils of illusion in the physical world, which have obscured their view of themselves and the Creator for thousands of years. They are becoming aware of the manipulation of the masses through fear and realising the truth of their own personal power.

Archangel Uriel helps us to move out of a state of duality in the third dimension and to view events from a state of neutrality.

As we break down the illusions created by the dogma and indoctrination into corrupt systems of control, we are able to rise above drama, observing duality from a greater perspective and integrating unity consciousness. At this level we are no longer immersed in that polarising energy and we become aware that there is no 'us and them' or 'left and right'. For, in truth, we are all one and everything just is. We see consciousness playing out on the great stage that is Earth and we are all actors playing our role in this great universal play.

When we reach the point of unity consciousness, we see that in reality the 'villains' are lost souls and that darkness is simply the absence of light.

There is only one way to deal with darkness and that is to radiate light and send it love. Love is indeed our greatest weapon.

Love transcends all.

How to Recognise an Illusion

Many of the beliefs you have about yourself are simply an accumulation of energy from past experiences, shaped by the mass consciousness and projections of others, creating limitations and boundaries within your reality.

When we view our beliefs as energy, they can easily be transformed into higher truths and altered or shifted completely. It is important to recognise that an illusion does not allow you to grow.

On the contrary, it takes away your power. This is a key way of recognising if something is an illusion or truth.

When you have released an old belief and recognised it as an illusion, you make way for more truth to flow to you. Information will find you; you will not have to search for it. Sometimes this information may be hard to accept as truth and you may question its validity, but call upon Uriel and he will continue to send you signs guiding you to truth. It may manifest as recurrent messages until you are ready to accept it, but each time it is presented, you allow yourself to gradually integrate this truth into your being.

In many ways discovering truth is a cycle of remembrance. Uriel will bring subtle reminders of truth over a period of time, so as not to overwhelm your mental and emotional fields. He will guide and support you in making space for a new, beautiful realisation to dawn. As you awaken to the truth of Source, you will feel deeply inspired with a new-found zest for life.

Due to the rising vibration of the planet and the higher frequencies anchoring onto the Earth, at this time many people are experiencing flashes of fourth- and fifth-dimensional energies coming through. It is almost like we are jumping in and out of different dimensional frequencies and we are physically feeling these effects in our daily life.

As a result, many of us are experiencing moments of great joy and alignment one day and then feeling extremely low, deflated and heavy the next. Uriel assures us that this is normal at this time of transition on the planet and describes it as an 'ascension symptom'. Rest assured all is well and as you elevate your awareness into the next level of consciousness, wonderful experiences will flow to you.

Here is a little summary of the different dimensions as I understand them:

Third dimension: The tangible, physical reality we now live in (most of the time). Separation consciousness, duality and polarity.

Fourth dimension: This is an in-between space that we often visit in our dream state; it acts as a bridge between the third and the fifth. In this dimension, thought manifests instantly so you have to be careful what you think of. In this space we are able to face our fears. It is almost like a training ground where we can prepare the mind for the fifth dimension.

Fifth dimension: Often described as 'the mind of light' this dimension is one of self mastery, bringing unity consciousness. In the fifth dimension, rapid manifestation through thought occurs as we step into the role of conscious creator serving the whole.

Healing Triggers

An important part of our ascension process is to connect with our higher multi-dimensional selves and to become the observer of our own human behaviours.

Our human third-dimensional selves will have many triggers, which are important to identify so that we can heal the energy behind them. By identifying and observing our behaviours and feelings around the trigger, we can shift into a neutral state and gain a higher perspective on the situation and the people involved.

Energy Analysis

Write down any individuals in your personal life that trigger you and why they trigger you. These are usually family members, friends, colleagues etc.

Now imagine being the observer and watching yourself reacting to this person. See everything as energy and know that the person who is the trigger is helping you to grow and evolve on a soul level. There may even be soul contracts or karmic debts at play here. See it from a higher perspective and next time you are triggered by this person, switch your emotion to gratitude for giving you the opportunity to learn and to grow.

Now that you have identified your personal triggers, think about any global triggers. (The common triggers in this category are usually centred around politics and public figures.)

Now imagine taking that bird's eye perspective and observing the collective consciousness. See everything as energy – see the dark threads of energy and see the light threads of energy. See that everything is interconnected and know that in this third dimension the light cannot live without the dark and vice versa. You can thank the trigger for playing its part in exposing the darkness. We have to be able to see it and pull ourselves out of polarity to break free from the illusion or the maya of the third dimension.

Discerning Truth

One of the greatest challenges of my metaphysical career was discerning truth after the shocking news that my former mentor and teacher, Doreen Virtue, had renounced her work and taken a complete 180, becoming a born-again Christian after having a vision with Jesus. One of the most alarming things that Doreen had said was that Reiki was extraterrestrial and not of the light.

This revelation sent me into a spiral of devastation and confusion. Both myself and my clients had experienced so many miracles through the angels and Reiki ... how could that possibly be wrong?

I went deep into meditation and called upon Archangel Uriel to help me discern truth. Uriel guided me to go to my local church to pray and ask for clarity. So, Doreen claims that Jesus appeared to her in a vision and, as a result, she denounced her work and teachings, but I had to remember that this was not my experience. I have my own relationship with the divine; I do not need Doreen to validate my beliefs or my connection to Jesus through her experience. I decided to ask Jesus directly to help me understand what was happening here. All of my being knew that something was not right, so I figured I would go straight to the man himself and ask the question.

I went to my local Presbyterian church on Mulholland Drive and sank deep into prayer. I asked God to send me a sign and if I was not on the right path then to please correct my course. I asked Jesus to show me the way and I also asked to get to know him better. I realised I had spent most of my time connecting with the angelic realms and although the angels are extensions of Source energy, it was now time to focus on connecting with God and Jesus directly. The truth is I was raised Catholic, but Catholicism always felt very fearful and so I had moved away from it. I often connected with Jesus in my healing sessions with clients. He is known universally as one of the great ascended masters and we can all learn from Jesus and his teachings no matter what religion or belief system we follow.

I realised that I hadn't ever really made an effort to get to know Jesus personally. I had, of course, listened to all the stories and parables and I have an A-level in Religious Studies, but if I'm honest I was just listening to a narrative that was preached over and over ... I had never even thought to dig deeper into the teachings of this amazing man that walked the Earth and made such an impact that he changed the world forever.

As I sat in church feeling so confused, I asked directly, 'Jesus, please guide me. May I get to know you better. Show me the way and give me a clear sign today, thank you.'

I left the church feeling a little lighter, trusting that my sign would come and bring clarity of mind. Before I got in my car, I looked out across the beautiful San Fernando Valley and gave thanks to Uriel for guiding me to come here in my search for truth. As I did this, my phone buzzed. It was a text message from a client I hadn't seen for a couple of years as she had moved to New York City. It read, 'Hey Katy, I hope you are doing great. My friend's dad is in hospital with leukaemia and he is looking for a Reiki practitioner. I told him you are the best! Can I pass along your number?'

In my then eight years of being a Reiki practitioner, I had never been asked to go into a hospital to do a session.

If I'm honest, I really do not like hospitals (who does?). They make me feel very uneasy with the stark bright lights, beeping monitors and machines. It's the least healing environment one can be in. In the future, hospitals will have lots of natural light and huge outdoor sanctuaries, healing salt lamps, crystals and healing sound frequencies alongside natural medicines … anyway, I digress.

When I read this message, I really did not want to go and, had I not just asked Jesus for a sign, I would have politely declined and recommended one of my students to go in. However, I knew there was more to this. I couldn't say no; if I said no, it would be through fear. If I said yes, it would be through love … so I said yes.

The lessons that would follow from this trip to the hospital were life-changing.

Before leaving for the hospital, I went outside to do a deep grounding and protection ritual. I knew I needed an extra boost and I literally looked up to the sky and said, 'Okay, I'm doing this because I know you're guiding me to do this, but if I'm going into that hospital I'm going to need a little extra help here God. Please surround me and protect my energy.'

As I sank into meditation, I connected with the earth and listened to the sound of the wind rustling the leaves overhead. I felt instant calm and I began to feel energy all around me. Then in my mind's eye I saw an energetic triangle coming towards me, followed by another and another, and so on. These energetic triangles were coming at me from all angles and then the penny dropped. I realised that a sacred geometric structure was being built around me called the merkabah, which translates literally to 'light, spirit, body'. The merkabah is said to provide protection and act as a light vehicle for soul travel, allowing your consciousness to explore higher dimensions. I didn't know much about the merkabah at this time, but I did know that it was powerful.

After this meditation, I felt strong and ready to go into the hospital to meet Joe. As I arrived at my destination in Tarzana, I realised I was half an hour early. Now, anyone who knows me knows that I am almost never early – I was 40 minutes late for my own wedding, for goodness sake! 'How strange I'm so early', I thought, 'hmm maybe there's a crystal shop I can go to before I head in to meet Joe.' So I Googled 'crystal shops near me' and, sure enough, there was one just around the corner. 'Perfect! I can buy some bloodstone to help Joe with his condition,' I thought.

Now I don't know about you, but when I enter a crystal shop I'm like a kid in a candy store. As I entered the store, I made a mental deal with myself to only buy the crystals for Joe and nothing else.

I picked out some bloodstone and as I walked towards the till, a book caught my eye on the top shelf. It was purple with a gold flower of life symbol on the cover. I felt drawn to it like a magnet. It was called 'The Ancient Secret of the Flower of Life' by Drunvalo Melchizedek. I stood staring at it hypnotised by its magical cover. My logical mind was screaming, 'Don't buy it, you're here for the crystals and only the crystals.' Still, I curiously reached up to touch the front cover and, as I did this, as if by magic, some leaflets fell out of the book dropping to the floor. I quickly picked them up and, upon further inspection, I realised that they were not leaflets at all, but actual pages from the book. I couldn't believe it; this had to be some kind of sign, I thought.

I proceeded to scan the pages and could not believe my eyes as there, as clear as day on the contents page of the book, was 'The Merkabah Meditation!' I gasped with utter shock and excitement and swiftly grabbed the book from the top shelf; my logical mind didn't stand a chance.

I left the shop with the crystals and my new magical book in hand. I could not wait to read it. I knew there must be powerful information in this book ... what a gift!

My hospital visit with Joe was difficult. I knew when I entered the room that he didn't have long on this Earth. As I set up a channel for healing and angelic connection, I realised that the reason for this meeting was not to bring about a miraculous recovery, but to help Joe with his transition to the higher planes.

I left feeling good that Joe had received this soothing, peaceful energy and that the angels were at his side. Joe seemed to be in and out of consciousness during the session and I wasn't sure if his physical self even knew I was there. When I arrived home, I received a message from Jeremy who was at Joe's side every day. Joe was like a father to him and it was Jeremy's idea to arrange the Reiki session. He texted me saying, 'Thank you so much for today, Katy. Joe told us that he loved the session and would like you to come again.' The next time I went to see Joe he was back home under 24-hour care, surrounded by his loved ones as he said his final farewell. I played angel music, called in all of Joe's angels and guides, and surrounded him with love and light. Not only did this make Joe's transition to the realms of spirit more peaceful, it also helped the loved ones surrounding him greatly as they felt the presence of our celestial helpers and took comfort in knowing that their dear friend was safe in the arms of the angels.

There were so many lessons learned from this experience and I am so grateful to Jeremy and my client Angela for reaching out, and of course to Joe for calling me to be of service in this way. On a soul level I was always meant to be there in his final hours for this beautiful exchange of information, wisdom and light.

There were so many levels of learning activated through my experience with Joe, and so much truth and wisdom that flowed from the merkabah meditation and the mysterious book that jumped off the shelf. The information within that book helped me to break many false beliefs I had been carrying my whole life; some were difficult to accept, but I called upon Uriel to help me discern the truth and I integrated that truth at my own pace.

My prayers have been answered in so many ways since that day that I went to church confused and lost. Not only did God teach me many things about the beautiful practice of Reiki and the angels, but my asking to 'know Jesus better' was a prayer that was answered in full force. Over the following months I was guided to learn more about Yeshua (Jesus's actual name in Aramaic, his spoken language) and his original teachings. As I studied the content of the dead sea scrolls, the gospel of Mary Magdalene and the Gnostic gospels, I would discover a whole new dimension to the incredible man that is Jesus Christ, along with the many hidden truths of the sacred feminine.

Thank you, Doreen, for helping me to accelerate along my spiritual path at a rate I could not have achieved without your influence. I learned many great lessons – to never put anyone on a pedestal, to be my own guru and to always discern truth based on my own direct experiences.

Meditation: Archangel Uriel's Pyramid of Truth

This is a meditation I channelled from Archangel Uriel that connects us to his pyramid of truth, clearing away false beliefs, helping us to think clearly and bring discernment.

It is also great for bringing laser beam focus to any projects we are working on.

- Take a moment to close your eyes and go inward.

- Take 3 deep cleansing breaths and say this invocation:

> *"Archangel Uriel please be with me. Please help me to break free from the shackles of social conditioning and indoctrination from the past. May I embrace a new, positive mind set and attract the truth in to my life. Please guide my spiritual discernment so that the truth resonates within my being. May you support and empower me on this journey to illumination."*

- As you take a deep breath visualise that you are sat in the middle of a magnificent golden pyramid.

- At the top of the pyramid is a powerful Ruby red crystal radiating light.

- You now see archangel Uriel appear before you with his magnificent golden wings of light.

- He creates a golden shield all around you from within this pyramid of light and dissipates old programming and false beliefs from your energy field.

- You surrender and release the ties of the past that have held you back for so long, as they are transmuted in to the light.

- Uriel sends a lightening bolt of golden-red light into the Ruby crystal capstone above, and a pillar of golden-red light extends down, connecting directly with your crown chakra.

- Feel this energy flow through your crown in to your head as this light illuminates your mind.

- Now asking that the wisdom from Source flow through this pillar and be integrated in to your soul.

- As you ground this wisdom and truth, the pillar of light flows through your crown, connecting all of your chakras as it flows through the centre of your brain, through the throat and in to the chest. Feel it filling the chest and activating truth and wisdom within your heart. Feel it flow in to the solar plexus, the sacral and all the way down to the root chakra at the base of your spine.

- Now feel the pillar flow through the ground beneath you connecting to all of the layers of the Earth and anchoring this truth and wisdom on to the planet.

- Give thanks to archangel Uriel for the light and wisdom you have received.

ARCHANGEL URIEL SUMMARY

Archangel of wisdom, lifting the veils of illusion, truth.

PRACTICES: Releasing false beliefs, discerning truth, grounding wisdom

COLOURS: Gold, Red

CHAKRA: Root and Earth Star
(part of the advanced chakra system)

CRYSTALS: Ruby, Pyrite, Tiger's Eye

CHAPTER 6

YESHUA

Let me give you a little insight into my experience of Jesus growing up in North West England. As a child, my dad would take me to church most Sundays, which I'm not going to lie, was a total snooze fest for a kid. The only thing that appeased me was taking my sketchbook and pencil. I would block out the dreary, monotonous tones of the priest, as I drew the angel sculptures and intricate patterns I could see on the stained-glass windows, getting lost in my imagination.

I find it fascinating that most of the world is indoctrinated into organised religion, without ever questioning what they are being told. If I think about my own upbringing as a Christian, I realise that I knew so little about Jesus himself. My main takeaways from going to church were that Jesus is the Son of God and if I don't live by Christian rules then I am a sinner, and if I am a sinner then only Jesus can save me, and if Jesus doesn't save me then the fiery pits await me … nice.

Oh, how this could not be further from the truth. If I'm honest, I almost feared Jesus growing up because of the perpetual scaremongering narratives played over and over, especially in Catholicism.

There was something deep-seated in Catholicism that always made me feel uneasy; an underlying darkness instilling fear and dread within me. Confess your sins to us they say, no sex before marriage they say ... err guilty; I had my daughter Gracie before I was married ... that makes me a dreadful sinner in the eyes of Catholicism. Thankfully, I don't buy into the fear one bit.

If I don't abide by these teachings, will my soul really be thrown into the depths of a fiery pit? Or is this man's flawed interpretation and manipulation of the scriptures in order to control the masses through fear? I can wholeheartedly say it is the latter. Thankfully, I have broken free from the dogma and indoctrination, and my awareness has expanded.

Now I want to be clear that I am in no way against anyone going to church. I occasionally go myself because I love the sense of community that it brings and I love most of the people I meet there. My aunty Pauline, one of the loveliest souls I have ever met, spent her whole life serving the Catholic Church and the community of Chester, England. She was even awarded the Benemerenti Medal by the Pope himself! She was an amazing woman, a true Earth angel, who inspired so many with her service to others. And I think this is what I love about churchgoers and the community – it should be about supporting each other and wanting to serve and help others. After all, one of Jesus's most powerful, yet simple, teachings was to 'love thy neighbour'. It is the fear narratives that I am against and the elimination of sacred truths, particularly those centred around the divine feminine ... and this isn't just in Christianity; it goes across all religions. My problem is with the handful of people at the top who pull the strings and decide what we are allowed to hear and what we are not. It's time for us to hear the full story.

It is time for us to hear the teachings of Jesus that they kept from us. It is time for the truth of the sacred feminine to rise, not only within religion but within the entire human collective.

As I embarked on my quest to learn more about the real Jesus, I could not believe the many layers to this great master that had been deliberately hidden from us. There is still so much to learn, but I would like to share with you some of the truths I have discovered through digging a little deeper into the written accounts of Jesus's life. Let's start at the beginning – Yeshua's birth …

We all know the story of the nativity: how Jesus was born in a stable and the three wise men came to honour him as the Messiah, but what happened after that? Why do we then suddenly skip three decades on to Jesus's ministry and crucifixion? In mainstream Christianity, we know hardly anything about Jesus's upbringing or childhood. Why?

The Bible says next to nothing about Jesus's formative years and astonishingly less than ten per cent of his life is covered in the New Testament. Jesus was crucified at the age of 33 and his short, yet profound ministry, only lasted for three years before his death. So, what happened in the 30 years leading up to this? What was he doing for most of his life?

Upon further research, I learned more about a very prominent figure in Jesus's life, who is mentioned very briefly in the story of the crucifixion when he stands before Pontius Pilate and claims Jesus's body for a proper burial. He is described in Matthew 27:57 as 'a rich man and a disciple of Jesus', and referred to in the gospel of Mark 15:43 as 'a respected member of the council, who was also himself looking for the kingdom of God'.

What the Bible does not tell us is that this man was Jesus's uncle, the brother of mother Mary. His name was Joseph of Arimathea and he was a very wealthy and well-respected businessman, a tin merchant who owned an entire shipping fleet.

You may be wondering why this is relevant, but bear with me. There are many accounts of Jesus in his earlier years travelling through Egypt, India and the British Isles with his uncle, giving us a greater insight into what his life really looked like. Some scholars suggest that Yeshua was raised amongst a secret and highly spiritual sect of society called 'The Essenes'. The first time I ever heard of the Essenes was around 2013. I was chatting about Catholicism to my beautiful and extremely intelligent friend Dr. Sarah Yeomans after a trip to Vatican City. Sarah is an exceptional archaeologist and historian who lectures around the globe on all matter of ancient history, including the early Church movement and the Roman Empire. To say she has an informed opinion on this topic would be an understatement.

Amidst our conversation about the Jesus portrayed by the Church, she informed me of a powerful truth when she interjected my general ramblings by saying, 'You do know that it's possible that Jesus was an Essene, right?'

'An Essene?' I said.

The word 'Essene' was so familiar, it was as though something had begun to stir deep inside of me … I knew it, yet I had never heard it before. It was like the word itself was so powerful; it held a whole other dimension within it, activating something that had lay dormant within my soul.

From that moment on I had an insatiable curiosity to learn (or remember) more about the Essenes and Jesus's connection to them. Sarah suggested I read a book called 'The Way of the Essenes: Christ's Hidden Life Remembered' by Anne and Daniel Meurois-Givaudan; a must-read for anyone on a quest for knowledge about the mysterious Essene community. My journey of discovery about the real Jesus was only just beginning and I could feel the ocean of my heart starting to stir as the waves of awakening came crashing over me, igniting the sacred fire of my soul.

The Essenes

Who were the secretive Essenes? There is much mystery surrounding this question, but let me summarise what I have learned so far.

For centuries before Christianity came to be, the Essene communities had dwelt on the shores of the Dead Sea. They were a Jewish sect, who had separated themselves from mainstream religion and society due to the deep-rooted corruption within the Temple and amongst the general public. Unlike the other sects of Judaism, the Essenes believed that Yeshua was the long-awaited Messiah. They had prophesied his birth for hundreds of years and had long been preparing for his arrival, creating a sacred community of highly evolved souls readying themselves to welcome Christ on to the Earth plane.

The Essenes were extremely intuitive and truly embraced their psychic abilities and gifts of foresight. They worked with astrology and the stars, and used a solar calendar as opposed to the more common lunar calendar.

They were known by many as 'The Children of Light' or 'The Children of the Sun' and lived very disciplined spiritual lives, honouring both the yin and the yang equally. Something that is very important to know is that the Essenes worshipped the Divine Mother and the Divine Father as one God, and this balance was reflected in their way of living and mutual respect for one another and the Earth.

Women were as important a part of the community as men and there were no restrictions or sanctions on women, like there are in the mainstream Judaic religions. Let's just pause and take that all in for a second …

> *'They worshipped the mother and the father equally as*
> *one God and women were equal to men.'*

Are you starting to see where we lost our way?

There were several Essene communes, one of which was out near the Judean desert in a place called Qumran and another at Mount Carmel in Israel, housing the Essene mystery school, which taught high-level initiates alchemical and esoteric practices passed down from the ancients. It is believed that both Jesus and Mary Magdalene were advanced initiates at this mystery school and went on to train at other mystery schools in Egypt and India.

There is a fascinating book by Dolores Cannon called 'Jesus and the Essenes,' in which she regresses a woman back to a past life where she lived in Qumran as part of the Essene community; the detail and accuracy of the regression is astounding! In this revolutionary book, it states that the Essenes taught meditation from the age of three upwards.

It was an integral part of daily life, practised every morning. The Essenes believed that morning meditation set a strong foundation for the day ahead and without that solid foundation, the energy would not flow and the day would be unharmonious.

I love this perspective. Imagine how different the world would be if we had been taught meditation from such a young age. In the words of the Dalai Lama: 'If every eight-year-old child is taught meditation, we will eliminate violence from the world in one generation.'

In his book 'The Law of Light: The Secret Teachings of Jesus,' Lars Muhl talks of Jesus being raised amongst The Essenes, who were great metaphysical teachers. He writes of how Jesus worked with astrology, studying the stars and planetary alignments, and that he often worked with crystals. Now I don't know about you, but I love a good crystal and I'm obsessed with star-gazing!

We also know for certain that Jesus taught to heal through the laying on of hands. As a Reiki practitioner, it is second nature for me to activate life-force energy to flow through the hands with the intention to heal. I believe that Jesus practised a form of energy healing. He knew that we each have the power to heal ourselves and others through the laying on of hands with a pure loving intention.

However, in the 1500s the Church went on to demonise such practices, labelling them as 'witchcraft'. The witch hunts began, resulting in hundreds of thousands of intuitive and highly spiritual women being burned at the stake … women just like me.

It is time to find our way back to the true teachings of Yeshua.

The Way

Before Christianity was called Christianity, it was known as 'The Way'. After the death of Jesus, those who followed 'The Way' were persecuted and hunted by the Romans, causing many to flee. This led to the disciples and apostles themselves fleeing Jerusalem and sailing to the South of France, where many went on to settle in the British Isles, upon the sacred Isle of Avalon, now known as modern-day Glastonbury.

There is a fascinating book called 'The Drama of the Lost Disciples' by historian and scholar George F Jowett, which gives a detailed account of the disciples' journey to Europe after the crucifixion. Jesus's Uncle Joseph of Arimathea transported tin and bronze all over Europe in his shipping fleet and had strong relations with Britain, particularly with the Druids, who had long awaited the birth of Jesus from their ancient and sacred prophecy of 'Yesu' (Jesus) as the Messiah.

When Joseph and many of the disciples, including his sister Mary (mother of Jesus), and Mary Magdalene, arrived in Britain they were warmly welcomed by the Druids and later gifted the Isle of Avalon as their home, where they went on to build the first Christian Church of 'The Way' in 37CE.

Whilst on my quest for knowledge about the lost wisdom of Jesus, I noticed that I kept seeing a specific symbol of two overlapping circles in my meditations. I frequently receive impressions in my third eye when meditating, and often it is like piecing together a puzzle to work out the meaning. I knew that the meaning of this specific symbol would be revealed in good time.

After all my research, I decided a trip to Glastonbury, in South West England, was in order, so I booked a lovely house for my sister and I overlooking the famous Glastonbury Tor. Settling into our new surroundings and tuning into the potent energy of this magical place, where feminine and masculine leylines converge, I realised how far I had come on my spiritual path. The last time I had visited Glastonbury was in 2008, when I partied hard at the legendary Glastonbury Festival. This trip would be a completely different experience to say the least!

My sister and I went on a soul-searching expedition around Glastonbury, visiting all the sacred sites, including the 'Jesus field' (many people claim they have seen apparitions of Jesus while walking across this magical piece of land), the Tor and, of course, the sacred Chalice Well. It was here that the meaning of the two overlapping circles became abundantly clear. For right there, laying over the top of the sacred well, which lay next to the ruins of the first original church of 'The Way', was an ornate covering featuring the two overlapping circles.

This ancient, powerful symbol, known as the Vesica Piscis portrays the sacred balance of the masculine and feminine. It is found at many spiritual sites around the world and is a prevalent symbol on the Isle of Avalon in Glastonbury. The Vesica Piscis represents the expression of creation itself, with one circle representing the Divine Mother and the other circle the Divine Father. Wow, how incredible to discover the meaning of my vision in this magical land, which holds so much wisdom and history relating to the life of Jesus. Everything was unfolding in divine ways as I embraced this new, exciting journey, discovering the lost teachings of Jesus.

Yeshua spoke of 'The Way' as the middle path of enlightenment, which is the perfect balance of the masculine and feminine energies within. This is the key to our ascension.

The Chalice Well, Glastonbury, England.

The Lost Teachings

As we have entered this new 2,000-year cycle on Earth, we are beginning to awaken to the ancient wisdom and truths of the past that have been hidden from us. It is no surprise that many of the scriptures containing Jesus's lost teachings are now resurfacing. Let's take a look at some of the fascinating discoveries over the past century, including the Nag Hammadi texts and the Dead Sea Scrolls, which just so happen to have been found in the Qumran Caves … the home of none other than the mysterious Essenes!

Allow me to summarise what I have learned about these powerful ancient scrolls. The Nag Hammadi texts were found in 1945 by an Arab peasant in a cave within the mountains surrounding the Egyptian village of Nag Hammadi. The texts were hidden in a large ancient jar around the year of 390CE, which happened to be the time of the Theodosian decrees. This was when the Roman Emperor Theodosius made Christianity the official state religion of the Roman Empire, banning any form of paganism, destroying temples and holy sites, and ordering the destruction of all materials not selected by the orthodox Roman Church.

Many of the books found within this sealed jar were written in the years just after the crucifixion by the disciples who studied with Jesus, and others are some of the oldest examples of leatherbound books ever to be discovered, with materials written up to 250 years before Jesus was even born.

Here are just some of the texts included in the Nag Hammadi library; The Gospel of Philip, The Gospel of Thomas, The Dialogue of the Savior, The Apocryphon (Secret Book) of John, The Apocryphon (Secret Book) of James, The Gospel of Truth, The Gospel of the Egyptians, The Apocalypse (Revelation) of Paul, The Apocalypse (Revelation) of Peter and The Thunder, Perfect Mind.

The first of the Dead Sea Scrolls was discovered in 1947, just two years after the Nag Hammadi texts. I mean that is some serious divine synchronicity right there. The scrolls were found in 11 different caves near the Essene community of Qumran. Written in Hebrew and Aramaic, some of them pre-date the birth of Jesus by over 100 years … just like the Nag Hammadi texts. These incredible scrolls make up over 800 texts written on tiny pieces of parchment paper.

Now stay with me as this is where it gets really interesting … these early Christian texts convey a very different Jesus to the one we hear of in Christianity today. They portray a more human, identifiable version of Yeshua, and reveal many of his teachings that the Church deliberately eliminated. This is why they desperately tried to conceal the findings of both the Nag Hammadi texts and the Dead Sea Scrolls, branding them as 'heretical and blasphemous'.

The Vatican kept the scrolls from being photographed or studied by anyone outside of their inner circle of scholars, who were instructed to 'safeguard the authority of the scriptures and promote their right interpretation'. Copies of the Dead Sea Scrolls weren't available to the public until over 40 years after their discovery!

What was it that they so desperately wanted to keep us from seeing? Well, brace yourselves … here is a summary of Jesus's teachings that they didn't want us to know:

- The Wheel of Karma.

- The multi-dimensional nature of the Universe.

- The unification of the masculine and feminine energies within one's heart and mind, leads to enlightenment.

- You are your own church and Christ Consciousness is within you.

- The existence of gods, archons and the demiurge (the false god that rules this world of illusion).

- Reincarnation is a universal truth.

- There is no original sin.

- There is no sin. In The Gospel of Mary Magdalene, sin is described as simply forgetting the truth, the divine nature of the soul, and then acting from that state. Sin is a mistaking of the ego for the true self.

- And last but by no means least … the existence of the Divine Mother.

PART TWO
GODDESS

PART TWO:

GODDESS

The truth of the Divine Mother has purposely been eliminated from our history books and religious texts. It has been hidden, burned and buried for thousands of years in order to oppress the mainstream and support man's obsession for power and control of the masses. This truth is now being unearthed and is rising once again into the collective consciousness. There is a paradigm shift happening on Earth and as the Goddess energy rises like a phoenix from the ashes, we realise that the gaping void within humanity is due to the elimination and desecration of the divine feminine.

The feminine aspect of the Creator has been completely disregarded by the patriarch. Most of us are only aware of the Father and the Son principle of the Creator, but did you know there is the Mother and the Daughter principle too? For the past 4,000 years we have only been taught one half of the equation; it is no wonder the planet is so out of balance.

The Creator is SO much more than we can ever imagine, the magnitude of Source is so mind-blowingly ineffable that there is really no point in even trying to describe Her.

Wow, as I write these words a magnificent thunderstorm is rolling in and lightning is flashing over the rolling hills of Wales – pure power! And, yes, I said 'Her'. For far too long we have been sold the idea of the Creator as male. I can assure you She is not male, He is a great androgynous force, presenting a perfect balance of masculine and feminine energy … but, for argument's sake, if He was going to be anything, then He would most certainly be a She, for the female aspect is the creative force, she is the giver of life and it was from the great cosmic womb of nothing that everything came to be.

It is time for us to unite and integrate this truth as we evoke the formidable energy of the cosmic mother, bringing balance to the divine masculine and feminine within our body, mind and spirit. This was one of Yeshua's greatest teachings … in order to walk the middle path of enlightenment, we must unite the sacred masculine and feminine within. On that note, I would like to introduce Yeshua's divine feminine counterpart, his closest companion and disciple, known as the 'Apostle of the Apostles' and described by Jesus himself as 'She who knows the all'; it is none other than Mary Magdalene.

CHAPTER 7

MARY MAGDALENE

Mary Magdalene is a powerful aspect of the Divine Goddess, honoured by many cultures across the world. She is a figure of much debate amongst religious scholars and her story is an important one to tell because it echoes the stories of women across the world and helps us to further understand how the Divine Feminine has been desecrated and disrespected by a self-serving patriarchal society.

Did you know that Mary Magdalene has her own gospel? You wouldn't be alone if the answer is no; it is never spoken about in church and the lengths that were taken to conceal it from us are astounding.

There is so much that has been hidden from us about this incredible woman, so many lies that have been told about her, so many truths that have been buried, but why?

By burying the truth of who Mary Magdalene really was, the patriarch could continue to rule, control and claim superiority over the matriarch, perpetuating the oppression of not only women but of the divine feminine aspect of God that lies within every human being.

The powers that be also knew that by concealing the truth of the sacred feminine, humanity would never be able to reach self-mastery and enlightenment, and could therefore be easily controlled. In the unification of the sacred masculine and sacred feminine energies, we activate the true essence of the soul and of who we really are – a perfect balance of both.

The Gospel of Mary Magdalene

The gospel of Mary Magdalene is the only gospel, that we know of, written in the name of a woman. It is not a part of the traditional Bible, nor is it ever referred to in mainstream Christianity. Being raised Christian myself, I had never heard anything about the gospel of Mary in church when I was growing up. I only remember Mary Magdalene being spoken of as a forsaken woman, a prostitute, whom Jesus forgave and redeemed.

On that note, I want to point out that Mary Magdalene was NOT a prostitute. This was something that the not so right and honourable Pope Gregory decided in the 6th century. He interpreted that an unnamed sinner in the Gospel of Luke was Mary anointing Jesus's feet and in order for the sinner to afford this expensive oil, she must have participated in 'forbidden acts of the flesh'.

From the 6th century onwards, the Christian Church has told the false tale of Mary Magdalene being the 'penitent prostitute', demoting women from having any form of authority within the Church for the last 2,000 years.

This unsubstantiated lie also aided in marginalising women everywhere and casting them into a position where they had to conform to the church's dualistic archetype for women, being either the virgin or the whore.

In 1969 (1,378 years later) the Christian Church officially corrected this mistake and revoked the interpretation of Mary Magdalene as a prostitute, but it was too little too late; the story of Mary being the 'sinful whore' was too deeply engrained into the collective psyche of Christianity. If you ask people today about Mary Magdalene, the vast majority still believe she was a prostitute – what a travesty!

Mary's story represents the unjust oppression and desecration of the feminine across all major religions and cultures across the world. It is time to put right the wrongs, to expose the lies, and to unveil the truth so that the sacred feminine may rise up and restore peace and balance to the world.

The Bible

If we look back to when the current New Testament of the Bible was compiled, we can begin to understand how and why Mary's story was so grossly distorted. In 325AD the Emperor Constantine and the Council of Nicaea (all of whom were men) came together to decide which scriptures would be chosen to become a part of the canon, composing the present-day Bible.

If we think of how a movie is edited, with lots of scenes and characters being cut from the story, we can see how the all-male council cut away the scriptures that didn't support the controlling male agenda of the day. You guessed it – all those scriptures containing the stories of women in leadership roles (of which there were many) within Jesus's ministry and the early Church, along with any that detailed Jesus's exceptional relationship with Mary Magdalene, found themselves left to rot on the cutting-room floor, and later ordered to be destroyed.

In the year 367 AD all the gospels that had been eliminated from the canon and considered sacred and imperative to the early Christian movement over three centuries, were ordered to be destroyed by the Bishop Athanasius of Alexandria. Thankfully some rebel monks decided to disobey this order and instead preserve and bury several copies in urns in the desert. Others were hidden away in caves, some of which would be rediscovered almost 2,000 years later, relating a very different Jesus to the one known within the Church.

One precious copy of the gospel of Mary was recovered in 1896 at an antiques market in Cairo, written in Coptic on ancient papyrus. Disturbingly, there were two major sections missing - the first six pages had been removed along with four pages in the middle, which equates to over half of the gospel, given that it was only 17 pages long in its original form. What was it that they so desperately wanted to keep from us?

Two small third-century fragments of the Gospel of Mary were later found, one in 1917 and the other in 1938. Both were written in Greek and authenticated the original gospel found in 1896. Sadly, the fragments did not reveal any more information than what was presented in the original copy, leaving us only with our imagination to fill in the blanks.

In 1945 the revelatory Nag Hammadi scriptures were discovered. Although there were no copies of Mary's gospel found amongst these early Christian texts, there are many references to Mary Magdalene and her unique relationship with Jesus, perhaps helping us to fill in the blanks of what may have been in those missing pages. Interestingly two of the texts that were bound with the first discovery of Mary's gospel, were also amongst the Nag Hammadi scriptures: The Apocryphon of John and The Sophia of Jesus Christ. These newly discovered texts are commonly referred to as The Gnostic Gospels, deriving from the word 'Gnosis', which in Greek means 'inner knowing' or 'knowing through direct experience'.

In the book 'Mary Magdalene Revealed,' author Meggan Watterson says, 'From a theological perspective, Mary Magdalene's gospel is considered an "ascent narrative", which means that it describes a path that we can navigate to liberate the soul; not in death, but here in this lifetime. The word ascent, though, is misleading in that the imagination immediately goes upward and thinks transcendence. Ascension according to the gospel of Mary is more accurately a descent into the heart; so farther up is actually further in.'

In the Gospel of Mary Magdalene, Mary contradicts the mainstream narrative of the Church by teaching us that there is no sin, we are each our own judge, and that we must embrace our human self and this beautiful journey that is life. She teaches us to see the light that exists eternally within us, the light that is us, and how to rise above the perpetual distractions of the ego and its tall tales, thus allowing ourselves to truly breathe in the joy of the present moment.

Mary Magdalene is there for anyone who calls upon her, regardless of their religious or spiritual beliefs. She is a powerful face of the Goddess and will help you to unlock the mysteries within your heart, accelerating you on your journey to ascension. Your heart is a portal and you can access other worlds and dimensions by tuning in to this portal. This takes time and practice, so be patient with yourself. To open the eye of your heart is to see through the illusions and know that everything lies within you.

Mary was also known as 'Mary the Magdala,' which means 'Mary the Great,' and like Yeshua, she was also raised amongst the Essenes. The Essenes believed Mary Magdalene was an aspect of the Holy Shekinah, the spirit of the divine feminine and the Goddess Sophia incarnate. We will learn about the great Goddess Sophia later, but first let's connect back to the celestial spheres so I can introduce you to some more of my favourite archangels.

The Divine Feminine Archangels

It is widely assumed that archangels are masculine; no doubt a product of our patriarchal conditioning. However, I want to reiterate that in truth angels are genderless beings of light; they simply carry a predominantly masculine or feminine vibration and really it is open to the individual's interpretation – there is no right or wrong.

However, this book is all about balance and I want to give you my interpretation of the archangels through my own direct experience.

Allow me to introduce to you four incredible divine feminine archangels; Gabriel, Ariel, Haniel and Jophiel. These beautiful celestial beings emanate a divine feminine energy around me that is so powerful and nurturing and I am so grateful for their continuous guidance and light. I am excited to share with you the phenomenal direct experiences I've had with them over the years in both my personal and professional life.

Remember each archangel carries their own frequency of light, which manifests as colour, and you can connect to these specific archangels through visualising their unique colour.

Here is a colour guide for the divine feminine archangels:

Archangel Colours

Gabriel

Ariel

Haniel

Jophiel

CHAPTER 8

GABRIEL

Speaking your truth,
divine communication, parenting.

Colours: White, rose gold, copper

Archangel Gabriel is one of the most well-known archangels.
Her name translates to 'God is my strength' and she is often depicted
holding a lily, representing rebirth. Most famous for her appearance to
the Virgin Mary in which she annunciated the forthcoming birth of
Jesus, Gabriel is known as the great messenger of the divine and appears
frequently in many of the scriptures across all major religions. She is one
of only two archangels mentioned by name in the New Testament; the
other being Archangel Michael.

Gabriel consistently delivers divine messages to humanity, acting as
a great mediator between the higher planes of existence and Earth.

Archangel Gabriel works on the white ray of light and sometimes emanates a rose gold/copper light. Many people think of Gabriel as male, but for me Gabriel has always had a very nurturing, feminine vibration. Interestingly Gabriel is portrayed as female in early Renaissance paintings, but over time she was more commonly portrayed as male, coinciding with the oppression of women. Why are we not surprised?

She helps artists, writers, public speakers and anyone who has an important message to share. I have actually called upon her to help me write this book!

Gabriel is excellent in assisting with any issues relating to children – anything from conception and fertility to adoption and parenting.

I had a profound experience with Gabriel when I was substituting a class at a beautiful meditation studio called Soul Hum in Los Angeles. Only two people showed up for class that day, so I decided that I would do a semi-private Angelic Reiki healing and a guided meditation with archangel Gabriel. Both women had profound but very different experiences. One lady called Barbara was having a particularly tough time with her teenage son and needed some deep healing and support with parenting. The other lady, Jane, didn't give a specific intention, but just lay back to soak up the healing vibes. However, whenever I connected with Jane throughout the session I was given a vision of a bridge of light – on one side of the bridge was Jane lay down on the meditation bed here on the physical plane, and on the other end of the bridge were eight or nine orbs of light playfully bouncing around. I was a little confused by the vision, as ordinarily I would have interpreted these orbs as spirit babies but there were so many of them and this threw me.

As the class came to a close, we gave thanks to Archangel Gabriel and all of the celestial beings helping and healing during the meditation. Both women were moved deeply by the experience and could palpably feel the angelic energy in the room; it was electrifying.

I felt compelled to tell Jane about the vision that I had seen for her, so I built up the courage and approached her, 'I have to tell you Jane, there is a lot of energy around you. I had a vision of you with a bridge of light connecting you to eight or nine beautiful orbs. The orbs seemed playful; they are connected to you somehow.'

I wasn't prepared for what Jane would say next. She looked at me, her eyes filled with both pain and joy, 'I have lost nine babies,' she said.

Gabriel was the bridge connecting Jane to her spirit babies and Gabriel was also the bridge for me to receive the vision and channel the message. It is moments like these that make me so grateful to be walking this spiritual path and helping others to connect to their light. Thank you, Gabriel.

Opening the Throat Chakra for Divine Communication

Gabriel is an extremely powerful guide for communicators and anyone who has an important message to share. We can invoke Gabriel to help us release fears related to teaching, public speaking and for performances that have a positive message to convey. She will help us to communicate from an authentic place, detaching from the ego, embracing our higher self and guiding us to speak our truth with love and power.

Take a moment to close your eyes and focus inward. Take a nice deep breath and say this invocation:

'Archangel Gabriel, please be with me. Please allow me to be a divine channel for communication. May you support and guide me to speak my truth with love and power.'

- As you take a deep breath in, visualise a spark of diamond-white light in your throat chakra.

- As you continue to breathe deeply, allow this light to grow and expand creating a beautiful orb of pure white light at the centre of your throat chakra.

- Archangel Gabriel now sends a beam of diamond-white light into your crown. Feel this beam of white light flowing through your crown chakra and connecting into the orb of light at your throat.

- You are now a clear channel of light as you communicate your message with divine flow.

- Give thanks to Archangel Gabriel and say this affirmation out loud:

'I am ready to speak my truth with love and power.'

Healing the Inner Child

As well as helping us with parenting and anything related to children, Gabriel can help us to heal our inner child. Often events that happened to us in our childhood will remain locked away and never dealt with; this creates blocks within our energy system, which in turn creates dis-ease.

This can manifest as mental imbalance through repetitive negative thoughts, lack of self- love and self-sabotage.

There often comes a time when we realise we cannot bury the past within ourselves any longer and it is time to release trauma and to forgive ourselves and others for their wrongs. It is important to know that however painful and traumatic an experience may have been, it has helped your soul to evolve and grow on many levels.

The soul will reincarnate over many lifetimes to experience different realities and grow from each one. I believe if we do not conquer our vices and overcome the challenges in one particular lifetime, then we face the same challenges and vices in subsequent lifetimes until we master them. Dolores Cannon talks about this concept in more depth in her book 'Between Death and Life.'

There is a very powerful healing visualisation that we can do with Archangel Gabriel to remove past traumas and energetic blocks from childhood. No matter what the experience may be, Gabriel can help us to identify the blockage and release it, starting the healing process and allowing us to expand and awaken to new levels.

Self-care is an essential part of healing wounds of the past. Allow yourself to take time to heal by listening to the following meditation and completing the exercise. Go to **katysloane.com/CGR**

You can do this angel ritual by yourself knowing that you are surrounded by a team of light as Archangel Gabriel takes you on a journey of healing to nurture your inner child.

Meditation: Healing the Inner Child

Get comfortable and close your eyes. Take a nice deep breath and say this invocation:

'Archangel Gabriel, please cradle my inner child in your wings of light, allowing me to release and heal the wounds that I have carried for so long.

As you heal and hold me in your light, please free the inner child within. Thank you, Gabriel.'

- Now, placing your awareness in your chest, imagine there is a beautiful diamond-white spark of light in the middle of your heart.

- Breathing deeply, see this light expanding with every breath.

- Gabriel beams light into your heart and you see this light begin to swirl, creating a diamond white vortex of light.

- Gabriel places her hands of light over your heart and you feel great warmth and love radiate throughout your entire body.

- The vortex burrows deep into your heart, creating a powerful tunnel of light.

- Now imagine yourself standing at the entrance of this tunnel. Gabriel appears at your side and guides you to step into it.

- You slowly begin to walk down the tunnel of light, travelling back through the timeline of your life.

- Become aware of any memories that may come into your mind as you continue to walk deeper into the light of your heart.

- You now notice that there is a beautiful glowing doorway at the end of the tunnel.

- As you approach this doorway of light, the silhouette of a child appears before you and as you draw closer you see that this child is you.

- As you stand before this beautiful soul and look into the eyes of your younger self, you feel great love and compassion for this child.

- You place your hand upon the heart of the child and say 'I love you'.

- As you look into the eyes of your inner child, you realise that every bad thought you have ever had about yourself has hurt this little soul. You realise this child is your very best friend, always there for you, never leaving you.

- Breathe deeply as you forgive yourself for times you have mistreated your inner child.

- Embrace this beautiful little soul that stands before you as Gabriel dissolves any blocks to self-love.

- Now look your inner child directly in the eye and place one hand on their heart and the other hand on your heart and say aloud, 'From this day forwards, I promise I will protect you, I promise I will treat you well and love you unconditionally, embracing all of your beautiful imperfections and seeing the radiant grace and beauty of your soul. I forgive myself for all the wrongs I have done to you. I love you, thank you. We are one.'

- Your inner child steps forwards uniting with your present self. Feel this beautiful fusion of energy and love as you become one.

- Gabriel now lifts you in her wings of light, back through the tunnel and into the shimmering white vortex, travelling back through the portal of your heart. You are now united with your physical body.

- Take a moment of gratitude and give thanks to Archangel Gabriel for this deep healing.

- Take a nice deep breath in and slowly wiggle your fingers and your toes, bringing your awareness back to the physical and slowly opening your eyes.

Listen to this meditation at **katysloane.com/CGR**

Don't forget to make notes in your journal about any messages, thoughts or feelings that came through in your meditation.

After the meditation:

- Take a moment to think about any visions of yourself that came through. What age or ages did you see yourself as?

- Were there any memories of other people from the past that came through in your meditation? Write down whoever came to mind.

Think about the relationship you have with yourself. Try to observe your thoughts and attitude towards yourself. Would you talk to your best friend or a child this way? If the answer is no (which it usually is), then remember your inner child and every time you become aware of your destructive self-talk, visualise sending love to your inner child as you pivot your thoughts to loving ones.

Tip: Find a photograph of yourself as a child and keep it on your mirror or somewhere you will see it every day. It is a great reminder to be kind to yourself.

ARCHANGEL GABRIEL SUMMARY

Archangel of speaking your truth, divine communication, parenting.

PRACTICES: Healing the inner child, receiving messages of guidance

COLOURS: White, Rose Gold, Copper

CHAKRAS: Throat, Crown

CRYSTAL: Clear quartz, Diamond, Sunstone

CHAPTER 9

ARIEL

Connection to Earth and animals, grounding, manifesting abundance.

Colours: Pink, magenta

Archangel Ariel is a divine feminine powerhouse; known as 'the Lioness Archangel', she has a fierce energy, bringing courage and strength to all those who call upon her. She is a stewardess of the Earth and radiates a protective, compassionate and grounding energy.

Ariel works on the pink ray of light and emanates a wide range of beautiful pink colours; from light pink to fuchsia, and even vibrant magenta. She connects us to the elemental realms, the animal kingdom and the healing force of nature. Ask Ariel for help with any environmental issues or assistance in healing injured animals or pets. She is a powerful guide for anyone who is involved in working with animals or conserving the environment and is fiercely protective of endangered species.

As the lioness archangel, she will often send signs to get your attention through dreams and visions incorporating the lion. She also delivers physical signs through pictures or references to lions, so keep an eye out for those and don't forget to keep track of any signs in your journal.

Ariel is deeply connected to the trees and urges us to ground our energy by venturing outside and taking in the beauty of nature, opening our senses to the joyful abundance that is all around us. Through this abundant mindset, Ariel will help you to manifest abundance in to all areas of your life, teaching you that you do not have to 'seek out' abundance for it is everywhere; you simply have to tune in to its frequency, bringing gratitude to the present moment.

Through this conscious connection to Mother Earth, she will help to ground our dreams into the physical, bringing abundance and prosperity. The Universe is gloriously abundant and, to receive, all we have to do is tune in to this frequency.

Ariel will assist you in becoming a conscious creator of your reality. For this reason, she is often referred to as the archangel of manifestation.

I have so many stories of how Archangel Ariel has helped me to consciously manifest amazing things into my life. She has helped me to become a master of manifestation, bringing great joy into my life through the art of conscious creation.

A powerful example of Ariel working her magic was in January 2020 (just before the madness of lockdowns hit), when I went to San Diego on a business weekend with my friend Liz.

We arrived at the fancy Fairmont Grand Del Mar hotel and couldn't
wait to see what this motivational business weekend had in store.

There were so many inspirational speakers and, as I watched them,
I realised that I already knew pretty much everything they were teaching.
It was a real eye-opener as it helped me to see just how far I had come
through years of metaphysical study and spiritual practice.

As I watched the speakers, I remember thinking how brave they were
to get up in front of all these people to speak their truth. As I had this
thought, Ariel came through strongly telling me that I would soon be
doing this too. I instantly panicked … there is no way I would be able
to get up and speak in front of all these people. 'Yes, you will!' Ariel said
– there was that lioness energy coming through again. As I was told this,
both fear and excitement flooded my central nervous system and I began
to visualise myself on the stage, empowering others to live their best life
and speaking my truth about connecting to the light and the celestial
realms. It was so strange. I was a little scared of this reality, but at the same
time I was visualising it and then her voice came through again. 'Courage,'
she said. I realised that this was the next step for me and I had to break
through the barriers of fear and channel my inner lioness. I asked Ariel
to oversee everything for the greatest good, knowing only that which
is aligned with my highest path would become manifest.

Two months later the world went into lockdown and what should
have been just a few weeks to 'flatten the curve' of Covid-19 turned
into over a year. I quickly forgot about the visualisation and the
message from Ariel that day until 18 months later, when the world
had finally re-opened, and I found myself back in San Diego.

This time on a well-deserved vacation with my family.

Whilst holidaying on Coronado Island, I received many incredible angel signs. For a start my room number was 1111! Then, whilst sitting on the balcony looking out across the stunning Pacific Ocean, I had an urge to check my emails. As I refreshed my mailbox, I could not believe what was there … I had received an invitation to speak at the Conscious Life Expo in London!

As I looked up from my phone, a huge white feather landed before me on the balcony – only then did it dawn on me that the last time I was in this beautiful place I had projected the vision of me speaking on stage and Ariel had told me this would happen. What a mind-blowing synchronicity to be in San Diego when I received the invitation to speak on stage!

The big day was soon upon me and on 19th September 2021 I gave my talk on ascension and awakening to your true power by connecting to the celestial realms, at the Conscious Life Expo in London, which was live streamed around the globe. Shortly after that, I was invited to talk at a special event in Los Angeles. The Universe had clearly decided that it was time to step out onto the world stage and start sharing my truth. Embracing the lioness energy of Ariel, I courageously seized the moment, overriding my fears with excitement and gratitude that this vision had now become manifest. Thank you, Ariel!

Manifesting with Ariel

Ariel will always oversee that your goals are divinely aligned with your life purpose. Sometimes we may believe we want things that are not necessarily the best thing for us, which is why it is so important to ask that these things come to us 'for the greatest good'. Often we can block a higher outcome from manifesting by obsessing over a specific thing; to avoid this, we can ask 'for this or something better' to manifest.

Goal Analysis

Go to your journal, or get a piece of paper, and write down your short-term goals. These are the things you would like to manifest over the next six months. Then write down your long-term goals, which are things you would like to manifest over the next five to ten years. Get specific. You can write down any tangible things that you want to manifest into being, such as a car, house, new phone etc. Or, alternatively, it could be a new relationship. Whatever it is, get clear and write it down and then move on to the manifestation meditation, below.

Meditation: Manifesting Dreams and Abundance

You can perform the following manifestation meditation for each of the things you have listed. Remember to really feel the emotion behind the goal in the meditation. How does it feel when you are receiving these things? How do you feel when you have achieved the goal?

Play the movie in your head as though it is happening in real life and imagine and allow yourself to feel into the moment of when these things are received and your desires become manifest.

Tip: The more emotion you put behind a goal, the quicker it will manifest!

Take a moment to close your eyes and go inward. Release any thoughts, worries or to-do lists; just be present in this moment. Take a nice deep breath and say this invocation:

> *'Archangel Ariel, please be with me and help me to*
> *open my channels of abundance. Guide me to manifest*
> *my dreams and desires for the greatest good, creating*
> *abundance and joy across all areas of my life. Thank you.'*

- Now relax, breathe deeply and imagine you are lay in a beautiful clearing. The blades of grass touch your fingers and you feel deep gratitude to be here, surrounded by the trees and nature.

- As you relax deeper, you see that a beautiful magenta pink light emerges from the surrounding woods, followed by many birds and butterflies.

- This light draws closer and you see it is a stunning angel gliding across the clearing.

- You feel a soft, warm breeze across your skin as this heavenly angel stands before you, emanating a powerful magenta pink light.

- This is Archangel Ariel. She has come to open and enhance your channels of abundance and connect you to the earth.

- She envelops you in her wings of light and guides you across the clearing, filled with wild flowers and butterflies.

- You enter the surrounding forest and before you is a magnificent ancient oak tree emanating light. It is strong and sturdy, with roots that burrow deep into the earth. Ariel guides you to sit and lean against its strong, sturdy trunk.

- As you connect to the magical energy of the tree, she tells you that this is your tree of life. Everything about your life flows through this tree – every interaction, every relationship is held here in the branches, and you realise that everything you have ever experienced has helped you to grow, to learn and to evolve. You give deep gratitude for your life so far.

- And now Ariel projects a screen of light before you and she asks you, 'What do you want to create in your life?'

- You see yourself appear on this screen of light and you see the things that you want to manifest appear before you.

- Watch these scenes play out on the screen and feel the joy and elation that it has come to be. Really feel the emotion as you receive those things you want most.

- Ariel now rolls these beautiful scenes into a scroll of light and says, 'this, or something greater, will manifest into your life'. She places the scroll into the trunk of your tree of life and you feel your energy has merged with the tree.

- Feel your energy flow from the crown of your head to the base of your spine and into the earth, connecting and uniting with the roots of the tree.

- As your energy becomes at one with the roots, feel them flow deeper and deeper into the earth. Feel them flow through the soil, in through the rocks and mineral kingdom, into the molten magma and through to the central core of the earth.

- Connect with Gaia, the consciousness of mother earth, and anchor to her light. You are grounded.

- Now bringing your awareness back to your physical body, slowly feel the energy in your hands and your feet and take a nice deep breath in through the nose and out through the mouth.

- Take a moment of gratitude and give thanks to Archangel Ariel for opening up the channels of abundance and connecting you to the abundant earth as you ground your dreams into being.

Listen to this meditation at **katysloane.com/CGR**

ARCHANGEL ARIEL SUMMARY

*Archangel of connection to Earth and animals,
manifesting abundance, grounding.*

PRACTICES: Healing Earth and animals, manifesting
abundance, grounding dreams into being,
connecting to Gaia (Consciousness of earth)

COLOURS: Pink, Magenta

CHAKRAS: Heart, Root

CRYSTALS: Rose Quartz, Pink Tourmaline

CHAPTER 10

HANIEL

Cosmic connection, moon cycles, intuition.

Colours: Turquoise, silver

Archangel Haniel is known as the Archangel of Joy and Grace. Her name in Hebrew translates to 'Joy of God' or 'Grace of God'. Bringing new insights, Haniel helps us to zoom out and take a higher perspective on things, enhancing our intuition and guiding us to reconnect with Source.

An important role that Haniel plays in the grand plan of creation is to connect human beings to the celestial spheres, including the stars and planets, which all have consciousness. She guides us in expanding our awareness and helping us to connect with the Cosmos and the energy of various planetary alignments.

Haniel is also very connected with the energy of the Moon and Venus and helps us to bring balance into our lives through tuning into the Moon's cycles. She particularly supports women, helping them to harmonise the physical and emotional bodies, balancing hormones and monthly cycles with the receding and renewing pull of the moon.

All we have to do is ask her for help and invite her in with a short invocation such as this:

> 'Archangel Haniel, please be with me and help me to balance my emotional and physical body as I tune in and align with the cycles of the Moon. Thank you.'

Archangel Haniel and Ariel often work in unison together – they are quite the dynamic duo, with Haniel guiding us to dream with the intelligence of the stars and Ariel helping us to ground those dreams into the physical.

I will never forget when I called upon these two amazing Archangels in my time of need back in 2017.

I had rented a house in Santa Monica for five years with my husband and two young children. We loved our little adobe-style house, just 14 blocks from the ocean. In July of 2017, I unexpectedly received a phone call from the landlord telling us that she planned on demolishing the house so she could build a bigger more contemporary home that she would live in. We had just three months to find somewhere to live. We were so sad, as not only did we love the home where we had so many great memories, but we had also said that the next time we moved it would be to a house that we would buy. 'Your word is your wand' as I tell all my clients! However, with only three months until move out date, it seemed highly likely we would have to rent again.

I reminded myself that this was the Universe forcing our hand and moving the chess pieces so that all could align for our greatest good. A month of viewing rentals went by and nothing had aligned … I decided it was time to take control and really call in the help.

With the solar eclipse fast approaching, Haniel was the perfect angel to call upon. On the day of the eclipse I headed to the ocean with my daughter, Gracie, where we wrote on a piece of paper that we wanted to manifest our new home quickly along with some of the key things we wanted our house to have … a garden, a pool and a hot tub were our specific requests.
 On August 21st, 2017, Gracie and I sat by the ocean and did a meditation visualising our dream home. We asked Archangel Haniel to empower our vision with the magical energy of the eclipse and asked Archangel Ariel to ground the dream into reality, overseeing that everything manifested for the greatest good. When manifesting, I always say:

*'May this manifest for the greatest good and if not this
then something better.'*

The next day I was walking my baby boy, Lennon, around our Santa Monica neighbourhood, when I bumped into a realtor called John. He was outside a beautiful house, making notes. 'Is this house going on the market? I asked, to which he peered at me from under his glasses and said, 'Yes, why do you want to buy it?' The conversation flowed from there and I explained the situation we found ourselves in with our rental house about to be demolished.

The next day John had arranged a meeting with a mortgage advisor, alongside several viewings. As I stepped into the third house, I instantly knew that this was our home. It had everything that we had asked for and it even had the same decor that was on my 'dream house' Pinterest vision board a year earlier!

After speaking to my husband, who was filming a show in Vancouver at the time, I arranged a virtual viewing for him. He loved the house too and after a rapid mortgage approval we put an offer in the next day. Just two months later we got the keys to our new home. Wow! I couldn't believe how everything had just fallen into place – like when has buying a house ever been that easy? Especially in Los Angeles, where people have bidding wars over houses – it was truly miraculous.

Thanks to Haniel and Ariel the stars had aligned for us and our dream home became manifest at lightning speed! Thank you Haniel and Ariel!

Manifesting and Releasing with the Moon Cycles

Did you know we can harness the energy of the Moon to help us reach our goals? The moon can aid us in releasing all that no longer serves us, as we surrender to the greater cosmic plan. Haniel encourages us to tune into the different phases of lunar energy, teaching us to build the energy and light around our goals with the cycles of the Moon, so that we can walk our highest path. Let's explore the Moon's phases and how we can apply the energy of each phase to our own lives.

New Moon

The New Moon is symbolic of new beginnings. It is a time to start new projects and embark upon new journeys, but it is also a time to reboot and mentally purge unwanted thoughts and emotions as you create a clear channel within yourself to focus on what it is you really want.

The New Moon is the phase of the lunar cycle when we project our wishes out to the Cosmos and believe with our hearts that they will become manifest. Allow Archangel Haniel to guide you and empower this ritual.

Manifesting with the New Moon

There are seven steps to successfully manifesting with Archangel Haniel and the New Moon:

1. Write your wishes down on paper (the power of the written word magnifies our intention).

2. Read the wish out loud under the New Moon (the power of the spoken word magnifies this further).

3. Play a mind movie of your wish coming true and really feel the emotion behind it, as your dream becomes a reality. Visualisation beams powerful thought energy out to the Cosmos. Think of your thoughts as radio signals being received by the Universe.

4. Affirm in your heart that it is already done. Don't doubt it – the energy of doubt creates resistance, which pushes the dream away from you.

5. Ask Archangel Haniel to oversee your wish for the greatest good of all and then set alight your piece of paper with your wish written on it and allow the words to flow into the ethers.

6. End this ritual by saying 'Om Namo Narayani'. This means 'I surrender to the Divine Mother' in Sanskrit, which is known as the language of the archangels.

7. As you surrender and allow the wish to transform from earth and fire into ether, release and detach. Refrain from thinking about out how it will come to you, instead trust that everything will align in divine ways as the wish becomes manifest.

Waxing Moon

As the New Moon progresses to the Waxing Crescent Moon, it gradually builds its light and energy. This should mirror the build-up of energy around the goals and intentions you set on the New Moon. As you take action and continue to have active faith in your dreams coming to fruition, momentum builds, bringing the desired outcome into being. Remember the more energy and emotion we put behind a goal, the quicker it will manifest.

Full Moon

The Full Moon represents fertility, transformation, completion and abundance. It is a powerful time to let go of all that does not support your highest good. This can be anything from personal relationships to negative emotions and destructive behaviours.

Haniel urges us to centre ourselves and connect to the energy of the Full Moon, using it as an opportunity to shed energetic blocks.

At this stage of the lunar cycle, emotions are extremely heightened and as we reach the Full Moon, a releasing ceremony is a great way to realign and balance your energy.

The Greek philosopher Aristotle spoke of the influence of the Moon on the human body, particularly the brain. The human body is made up of around 80 per cent water, with the brain being the most moistened organ in the body. The Moon, with its magnetic pull, influences all water on the planet, including that within the physical body. Interestingly, the term 'lunatic' derives from the influence of the Moon on a person's emotional state! Be mindful around the Full Moon, it is a time when lunar energy is extremely potent, magnifying our emotions. Try to remain neutral and avoid triggering situations at this time.

You can let go of any heightened emotions by writing your thoughts and feelings on paper and practising a releasing ceremony. This is very similar to projecting your intentions with the New Moon. Once you have written all that you want to release on paper, burn it under the Full Moon and watch the energy spiral into the ethers. This is extremely powerful and through this practice we can feel as though a weight has lifted.

Beware: if you don't release with the Full Moon, tensions can rise, magnifying thoughts and emotions that lead to irrational and negative behaviours.

Waning Moon

The Waning Moon is a good time for us to focus on releasing bad habits and stressors. As the light of the Moon gradually decreases, we feel a calmness as we consciously override negative thought patterns and enhance our communication with others. The Waning Moon can also be a time of revelations and breakthroughs as we endeavour to complete our projects.

In the third quarter of the Waning Moon, we see another Half Moon, but this time softer and decreasing in illumination. This is a time to stop, slow down and re-evaluate for the future. At this point in the lunar cycle, the seeds have been planted and grown and the harvest reaped.

Haniel guides us to contemplate and give ourselves praise and gratitude for our accomplishments as we focus on our highest path and look at things from a neutral, universal perspective. This gives us an open flow of energy preparing us for another beginning as the New Moon approaches.

As we move into the Waning Crescent Moon, Haniel urges us to detach from the world and rest. This is a time for self-reflection as you decide what things do not serve you and allow creativity and growth for the next stage of new intentions.

A new beginning approaches with the power of the New Moon.

Enhancing Your Intuition

Archangel Haniel helps us to tune into our third eye chakra to receive psychic insights, particularly through visions (clairvoyance) and feelings (clairsentience). She will help us to access higher levels of information and light, acting as an intermediary between human beings and the celestial spheres of wisdom in the higher realms. Haniel helps us to absorb and understand esoteric information and complex spiritual concepts and integrate them into our conscious mind, allowing us to translate them through language.

I have conducted many Moon meditations with Haniel and I have also entered into deep altered states of awareness with her, in which I have taken my consciousness to the celestial spheres. In these altered states I would often connect with the energy of the Moon and Haniel would guide me deep into the centre, which always seemed to be hollow. Within the hollow Moon was a special chamber where many beings gathered, and where there was a very large screen which acted as a viewing window to the Earth. In my soul travels to the Moon, I was shown that Earth was being monitored from within the centre of the moon … sounds crazy, I know!

Yet maybe it's not so crazy after all. You see, since these visions much information has flowed to me about the Moon. One of the big revelations I discovered is that the Moon is not a naturally occurring phenomenon and many scientists pose the theory that the Moon is indeed hollow. So aside from my crazy moon visions, let's look at what evidence we have to support this.

There have been many seismic experiments performed on the Moon that have created very interesting results. One of these was the Apollo 12 mission in 1969, orchestrated by NASA in which a seismometer was left on the moon.

Here are some key details of the experiment taken from solarsystem.nasa.gov: 'After docking with Yankee Clipper in lunar orbit and transferring into it for the ride home, they jettisoned Intrepid and set it to crash into the lunar surface to calibrate the seismometer they had left there … It hit the Moon at a speed of 3,735mph, this was 47 miles from the instrument, creating the first official moonquake. The result was unlike anything experienced on Earth. The vibrations didn't subside significantly for nearly an hour.'

Simply put, the Moon rang like a bell, suggesting that it cannot be the solid sphere of rock that we have been led to believe, but rather a hollow structure. Now, the legendary Astronomer Dr Carl Sagan, with his extensive research on the Cosmos, says, 'A natural satellite cannot be a hollow object.'

One thing that pretty much all scientists agree on is that the Moon defies the laws of physics; its size and distance to the Earth and Sun just doesn't add up.

As I dug deeper into the history of the Moon, I found much evidence to suggest that the Earth once existed without the moon. There are many ancient texts that suggest there was a time when the Moon was not in our skies. Aristotle spoke of the 'Pro Selenes', a race that existed before the Moon.

The Mayans spoke of Venus ruling the skies before there was a Moon and in Psalms, The Bible mentions that there was a time when the Moon did not shine! Is your mind blown yet? I know mine was … you live your whole life believing something to be true, only to find out it couldn't be further from the truth. Welcome to the journey of awakening my friend!

So, what is the mysterious Moon and where did it come from? Why was it put there and, more importantly, who put it there? These are all valid questions and, honestly, I am still figuring out the answers. Take time to go inwards, connect with Haniel and ask her questions. Uriel is also a great Archangel to call upon to help you to integrate truth and break old programming. Remember now is a time of great awakening on Earth and the angels are urging us to question everything!

As you expand your consciousness with Haniel, she will help you to understand the eternal nature of the Creator outside of time and space, allowing you to shift into Cosmic Consciousness, remembering your innate connection to the stars.

Intuition Rituals

Here are some exercises that you can practise to help you to tune in to your third eye and enhance your intuition. You can invoke the presence of Archangel Haniel to help you with each of these exercises.

Try a walking meditation: Intuition requires presence and a great way to practise being present is to do a daily walking meditation. As you walk out in nature, make it your goal to notice everything.

Practise being aware in the present moment, tune out all thoughts, focusing only on the beauty around you and how things look, smell, sound and feel. Most people walk around completely oblivious to the world around them. Our angels are always sending subtle signs and messages, which for most go unrecognised. The more you tune in to the present moment and notice everything – whether it be the intricate detail on the bark of a tree, the sound of the leaves blowing, or the colour and fabric of someone's coat – the more aware you will become and the more you will awaken to your intuition and truth.

Psychometry – the art of reading the energy of objects: Rub your hands together until they are warm (if you are attuned, activate your Reiki), and then hold an object between your palms. This could be someone's necklace, ring or keys. See what kinds of feelings arise and sense the energy of the object. You can also do this with crystals; simply tune in to the vibration of the crystal and see what messages you can download. There is no right or wrong with this exercise; you are simply strengthening your third eye and activating your intuition.

Automatic writing: Quieten your mind and think of something you would like guidance with. You can call upon Archangel Haniel and Archangel Gabriel to help you with this exercise. Now do a short ten-minute meditation. This can be something as simple as focusing on your breath while you listen to calming music, or to the subtle sounds that are around you. After meditating, sit down with a pen and piece of paper and think about what you have asked for guidance with. When you are ready to write, soften your hand and allow the messages to flow through the pen and onto the paper. Don't overthink things – surrender and allow the messages to flow. The more you practise this, the more you will expand this channel of communication and receive clear messages.

Meditation: Journey to the Sacred Moon

- Take a moment to close your eyes and go inward.

- Release any thoughts, worries or to-do lists. Simply be present in this moment.

- Take a nice deep breath and say this invocation:

  'Archangel Haniel, please be with me and help me to enhance my intuition, bringing divine insights and wisdom. Guide me to expand my awareness and align to the energy of the Cosmos, as I connect with the Moon, stars and celestial spheres. Thank you.'

- Imagine you are lying beneath the starry night sky and the Moon is shining down upon you. Absorb this cosmic light.

- As you relax deeper, you see a beautiful turquoise light appear in the centre of the Moon. It glows bright, expanding and enveloping the Moon with a turquoise halo of light.

- This is Archangel Haniel, emanating her divine feminine light from above.

- Haniel beams a beautiful pillar of light all the way down to the Earth where you are lay.

- You now become aware that there are many orbs of white light around you. These are your angels and guides. They are here to lift you into the celestial spheres of light.

- Feel your awareness lift from your body as the angels take you up the pillar of light.

- As you rise up out of Earth's atmosphere, you look back from your higher vantage point and see the beauty of your planet.

- Rising higher, you see the stars and the spiralling galaxies all around you and you feel at one with the Cosmos.

- Rising higher, you feel the soft light of the Moon illuminating your soul and, as you approach the surface, Haniel appears as a Goddess of turquoise light with incredible flowing silver wings.

- She greets you with love and envelops you in her wings of light.

- A tunnel now appears burrowing deep into the Moon.

- Haniel takes you into this tunnel of moonstone and you see a shimmering doorway of light at the end.

- This door opens to a sacred chamber of light within the centre of the Moon. You will now enter this chamber to receive important wisdom for your soul's journey.

- Stepping through the doorway and into the chamber, you see a beautiful mandala of light upon a glistening round crystal table.

- Haniel guides you to sit and place your hands upon the table, absorbing the crystal energy. There are many intricate carvings upon the crystal and Haniel tells you this is light language, absorb these vibrations of wisdom and truth.

- She tells you:

> *'There are great truths that have been lost for thousands of years; it is finally time for these truths to be revealed on your planet. Earth has entered one of the most important times in the history of the Universe. You are a light worker and you must stand strong as the control systems crumble and the darkness falls. Recharge in this scared chamber and take this Divine Feminine energy and light back to your planet.'*

- Lifting your hands from the table, you place one hand over your heart and one hand over your third eye, as the crystal Moon energy flows into your heart and mind.

- Now, feel the energy charging up your entire body, illuminating every cell.

- Haniel now tells you it is time to go back – Mother Earth is calling you.

- You enter back through the shimmering doorway of the chamber and into the moonstone tunnel.

- Approaching the end of this tunnel, you see the surface and observe the Universe from the vantage point of the Moon. All around you are star constellations, stardust, vortexes and portals.

- As you look into the infinite Cosmos, you feel the energy from all these stars and vortexes uplifting your soul, and you now see that there is an army of celestial light beings watching over your planet and beaming higher frequencies of light on to Earth.

- Haniel illuminates the turquoise tunnel of light extending back to your planet.

- You glide back down this tunnel and as you enter the Earth's atmosphere you see the oceans, mountains, rivers and valleys on your magnificent planet.

- You become aware of yourself lying on the Earth surrounded by light, as you connect back to the physical and place your awareness into your body.

- It is now time to ground this energy to the Earth. Placing your awareness in your root chakra, send a beam of light from the base of your spine into the Earth and see this beam connect instantly to the core of Gaia, anchoring to her light. You are grounded.

- Now feel the energy in your body, slowly moving your hands and feet, and take a nice deep breath in through the nose and out through the mouth.

- Take a moment of gratitude and give thanks to Archangel Haniel for the divine wisdom and energy you have received.

Listen to this meditation at **katysloane.com/CGR**

ARCHANGEL HANIEL SUMMARY

Archangel of grace, cosmic connection, moon cycles, intuition.

PRACTICES: Manifesting with the phases of the Moon, enhancing psychic abilities, integrating universal wisdom, empowering the divine feminine within.

COLOURS: Turquoise, Silver

CHAKRAS: Third eye, Throat

Crystals: Aqua Aura Quartz, Moonstone

CHAPTER 11

JOPHIEL

Beauty, artistic expression, connection to the Divine Mother.

Colours: Gold, yellow

Archangel Jophiel has a beautiful, calming presence. She works on the yellow ray of light and emanates a vibrant golden yellow energy. Her name translates to 'Beauty of God' and she is known as the archangel of wisdom, artistic expression and, of course, beauty.

When you invite Jophiel in to your life she will bring a sense of peace and harmony, helping us to calm chaotic situations, beautify our thoughts and bring mental order. She guides us to see the silver linings in all situations, creating moments of peace and joy even in the most difficult of times.

Jophiel will help to appease a turbulent mind and with an accumulation of 60,000–80,000 thoughts per day on average, we certainly need it.

If we want to create more beauty in our lives, it is essential to calm the mind and align our energy to attract abundance and joy. The best way to do this is to meditate every day. Through meditation Jophiel can help to soothe the mind, bringing clarity and allowing you to see the beauty all around you.

Our outer world is a reflection of our inner world and Jophiel helps us to understand this, as through our peace of mind, harmony can be restored within our surroundings. For this reason, she is often referred to as the angel of Feng Shui, helping us to be organised around the home, so that the energy can flow harmoniously.

A quick and easy visualisation is to call upon Archangel Jophiel and her golden cloak of light. This is extremely uplifting and will help to enhance your creativity, boosting your mood and self-esteem as you tap into the inner beauty of your soul and allow your light to shine.

Energy Ritual Invocation

'Archangel Jophiel, please bring me your golden cloak of light, boosting my creativity and bringing divine inspiration.'

- Take a moment to visualise yourself draped in a beautiful, shimmering golden cloak of light.

- Feel the golden energy flowing over you and covering every part of your body, all the way down to your feet.

- Finish by placing the hood from your cloak over your head as if you are wearing a physical garment made of light.

- Give thanks to Jophiel for her creative cloak of light.

Tip: This is a super-quick and easy visualisation for when you are up against the clock. You can use this exercise for other archangels too. Simply switch the colour and your intention to suit.

The Cosmic Ladder of Ascension

The cosmic ladder of ascension symbolises the different levels of spiritual attainment we must achieve to reach enlightenment. Archangel Jophiel guides us to climb this ladder, helping us to raise our vibration through spiritual practices and ignite the divine feminine wisdom within. With this comes a rebirthing and remembrance of who we really are, as we step into our power and gracefully rise through the different levels of consciousness on the cosmic ladder of ascension.

I had a profound experience with Jophiel in 2013 when I was organising my wedding day. It was an exciting time, but also very intense and stressful. Meditating was essential to keep me balanced and one particular day I decided to take an hour to lay on my bed and do some self-healing, along with an angel meditation. I called upon Archangel Jophiel to help me and drifted off into an altered state. Towards the end of the meditation, I became aware of intense waves of energy all around me, so much so that I opened my eyes to see if I could actually see anything.

As I opened my physical eyes, I saw a beautiful golden ladder of light above my body, extending up into the centre of the ceiling. I stared in astonishment – the ladder was there for around 10 seconds and then disappeared into thin air.

Several months later, on my English wedding day (not the Vegas one, ha), the Reverend read a verse from the Bible that spoke of 'Jacob's ladder' or 'the divine ladder of ascent'. She said that this ladder connects the angels to heaven and Earth. I instantly thought of my amazing vision of the golden ladder just months prior. To hear this explanation on my wedding day was such a gift. The angels sent me many miracles around the time of my wedding, which actually had an angelic theme!

When writing my angel courses a year or so later, I discovered that Archangel Jophiel's esoteric symbol is the 'Cosmic Ladder of Ascension'; this gave the vision of the golden ladder even more significance. It is common for us to receive messages from the angels, but not necessarily understand the meaning of the message at the time we receive it. However, so often the meaning will be revealed months or even years later.

Another miracle was sent to me exactly a week before my wedding. As a trained fashion designer, I had loved designing my own wedding dress and a week before the big day I got the phone call that the couturier had finally finished making my dress. I excitedly headed to London to collect it. However, when I got there I realised to my great dismay that there was no bridal belt to go with the dress ... this may not seem that big a deal, but the belt was key in pulling the look and style of the dress together.

I was so upset as without the bridal belt my dress felt incomplete, and at this point there was not enough time for one to be made. I would have to find one to buy with just seven days to go until the big day. Time to call in the help, I thought! There was one particular bridal belt I had wanted from the very beginning, by a designer called Manuel Mota for the label 'Pronovias'. However, these belts were extremely intricate and made by hand in Barcelona; they had to be ordered at least six months in advance.

I called every single wedding store imaginable to ask if they had any bridal belts available for me to buy, but I was met with the same answer every time, 'We can order one for you, but you won't get it in time for your wedding.'

Feeling completely deflated and so upset that my dress was not what I had imagined, I decided to take a moment and do myself an angel card reading. The 'Divine Mother' card flipped out instantly. It read, 'Expect miracles'. I must have thanked God a thousand times for this miracle that was yet to arrive. A miracle was exactly what I needed and I knew the angels were on the case and events were being orchestrated behind the scenes to solve my dress problem. Trust and let go, I thought.

Shortly after this, I left my house and headed to the petrol station to fill up my car. As I stood at the side of the pump, I looked up to the sky. It was lit with the most beautiful golden light as the sun was setting. In this moment I felt the presence of the Divine Mother as all the stress melted away and I was completely present looking at the golden sky. I once again gave gratitude for the miracle that was coming and got back in my car before noticing I had a missed call on my phone with a voicemail from a number I didn't recognise.

The mystery voicemail said, 'Hi Katy, can you call me back ASAP, I have some exciting news.'

I called back right away and a lady called Karen from a small independent bridal boutique answered the phone. She proceeded to tell me the exciting news: 'When you called earlier today, I felt so bad that we couldn't help you, so much so that I was telling my colleague about you and how upset you were that the belt was missing from your dress. Just at that moment the owner of the shop came in, which is really quite rare, and he overheard what I was saying.'

She continued, 'I told him your wedding was in a week so we didn't even have time to expedite you a belt. He then said he may be able to help and led us into the back of the shop into his office. He opened his desk drawer and pulled out a mysterious package. As he opened it, he said, 'This is a Pronovias belt that one of my private clients ordered but she decided that she preferred her dress without it. I've had it in my drawer for months and totally forgot about it until just now.'

My jaw dropped – not only was this a Pronovias belt, but it turned out to be the exact belt designed by Manuel Mota that I had originally wanted … it matched the design of my dress perfectly! I was absolutely speechless.

I thanked Karen profusely before asking her how she got my phone number to even call me. She said she had looked on the call log for that day and deciphered the time I called in order to get my number.

Wow, 'What a beautiful human being … or was she in fact an angel herself?' I thought. I excitedly drove to the small independent bridal store in Warrington, England, to pick up the belt. To this day I am so incredibly grateful to this lady for listening to her angels and picking up the phone to call me. I am also amazed that the angels had orchestrated these events even before I had known that the belt on my dress was missing. When I think about all the things that had to align for this to happen, I am stunned, it really was a miracle. Archangel Jophiel was working closely by my side throughout the planning and organising of my wedding, keeping me balanced and calm amongst the chaos. As the divine feminine archangel of beauty and artistic expression, she constantly supports me as an artist, bringing divine insights and inspiration. Thank you, Jophiel!

Jophiel and the Divine Mother

Archangel Jophiel is very connected with the divine feminine aspect of God and is particularly helpful in guiding artists and creatives to express their energy, especially at this time in humanity's evolution.

In the patriarchal society, the power of creative expression has been hugely undervalued. We have seen this with the defunding of the arts in mainstream education, depriving our children of their creative outlets and self-expression, which is crucial in aiding emotional balance. Often when children lose focus due to the constant pushing of logical left-brain learning, they are told they are not good enough or that there is something wrong with them, when in reality they simply need to be stimulated creatively to aid their focus.

Jophiel urges us to look deeper and assess everything on an energetic level. There must be balance for the soul to flourish, and children, especially, need daily creative outlets to balance and express their heightened emotions. Even if we do not consider ourselves to be artistic, Jophiel asks us to honour our divine feminine energy by allowing it to flow through creative endeavours, such as dance, art, writing or music. Part of Archangel Jophiel's mission is to help us to remember who we are and reconnect us to the Divine Mother ... the creative aspect of Source.

Activation with Jophiel and the Divine Mother

- Take a moment to close your eyes and go inward.

- Take a nice deep breath and say this invocation:

  'Archangel Jophiel, please be with me and surround me with your golden light. May your light flow through me, illuminating my heart and mind, and sparking my creativity, as I connect to the energy of the Goddess. Thank you.'

- Placing your awareness on your breath, continue to relax, releasing stress and tension on the outbreath.

- Imagine yourself sitting at the peak of a mountain. As you look out from the summit, you see the beauty of the Earth as the golden sun shines across the world.

- Archangel Jophiel appears behind you and envelops you in her golden wings of light.

- You begin to hear the sound of flowing water, as a stream of golden light cascades down the mountainside, flowing into the great rivers and valleys below and illuminating the vast ocean before you.

- White doves soar overhead, as the trees, mountains and oceans of earth are shimmering with golden light.

- You take in the beauty that is all around you and feel completely at one with all that is. You are a beacon of light, connected to the magnificent Earth below and the great celestial skies above.

- Suddenly you feel the Earth rumble beneath you as the mountain cracks and the golden light of Divine Mother rises from deep within the earth, streaming her light out into the heavens.

- You feel incredible energy surging up from within the Earth, as you are lifted off the mountain peak and into the cascading waterfall of light.

- As you descend down the mountain with this beautiful waterfall, you plummet into a great river below and are swept along with the golden light of the Goddess. Feel the powerful light codes activating your creativity, shifting you into a higher consciousness.

- The river merges with the shimmering ocean and you are now bathing in an ocean of calm. Take a moment to just be, knowing you are completely supported and held by the waters of the Goddess.

- You are completely immersed in this golden light as it cleanses your body, mind and spirit and attunes you to the sacred truth of the Great Mother.

- It is now time for you to enter a whole new chapter of your soul's evolution. The miracles of the Goddess await you.

- Take a moment of gratitude to Archangel Jophiel for this sacred light activation.

Listen to this meditation at **katysloane.com/CGR**

As we connect to the energy of the Goddess, prepare to awaken to new levels of truth and light.

The wisdom of the Divine Mother was taught in the ancient past by the great masters who walked the Earth. This wisdom has been buried and hidden from mainstream humanity for thousands of years. It is now time for these teachings to be heard. As the Goddess rises like a phoenix from the ashes, she is ready to guide us all into a new age of peace and harmony. Prepare to soar above the heaviness of the third dimension and enter into a new paradigm in which the teachings of the divine feminine are no longer secret but embraced and honoured, bringing balance to the hearts and minds of humanity.

JOPHIEL SUMMARY

Archangel of beauty, artistic expression, connection to Divine Mother.

PRACTICES: Seeing the beauty in all things, empowering your creative self, honouring the divine feminine within, climbing the cosmic ladder of ascension.

COLOURS: Yellow, Gold

CHAKRAS: Solar Plexus

CRYSTALS: Citrine, Gold

CHAPTER 12

THE GODDESS SOPHIA

The divine feminine aspect of God is known by many as 'Sophia', which translates to 'wisdom' in Greek. The early Gnostic Christians and those of the Jewish mystical tradition of the Kabbalah spoke of the imperative role that She plays in the quest for enlightenment.

It is easy for our human minds to think of God in a human form. I'm sure many of us can relate to the image of God as a man sat on a throne in the sky with a long, white beard. This is a common interpretation given to children raised into mainstream religion, but what if we think of God as a divine and formidable frequency that permeates all things?

Within the ancient Nag Hammadi texts, it states that the creator of the Universe is 'an aeon named Sophia'.

In these sacred writings, Sophia is considered to be a divine frequency represented through fractal energy. This directly relates to the golden mean ratio, a sacred geometric spiral which is found throughout all of creation, including our human DNA. The golden mean is based upon a universal ratio which represents the divine design present in all forms of life and matter.

If you look at the centre of a flower or the intricate form of a pine cone, you will clearly see the golden mean.

The light of the Creator flows through all that is, and it is now time for the divine feminine light of Sophia to ignite within us and rise up to dissipate the darkness. The all-encompassing energetic unified field that connects all things is Sophia.

As we connect to Goddess Sophia, she reminds us that everything is energy and that everything holds consciousness. Our DNA contains the golden light codes of Sophia, which have lay dormant but are now ready to be activated as you awaken to the truth of who you really are and ignite the light within.

How I Came to Know Sophia

Let me take you back a few years to when I first learned of the mysterious Sophia, and how I invited her into my life and watched many miracles unfold before my eyes.

In 2018 I was living in California with my husband and my children; Gracie, aged nine and Lennon, aged three, and our Golden Retriever puppy, Darla. The year before we had moved from Santa Monica to our dream house in Encino Hills, Los Angeles (you know the story), which meant we had to switch Gracie to our new neighbourhood school in the Los Angeles Unified School District.

The school had excellent statistics and was highly recommended by many people, so I enrolled Gracie and she entered into the third grade. Little did I know, over the next year and a half, I would slowly witness my daughter transition from a joyful, bright, shining light, to a sad, anxious and depressed little girl, a shadow of her former self. It was heartbreaking seeing her decline.

At the new school, she was constantly told she 'wasn't good enough', made to read her 'disappointing' grades out loud and shamed by being given neon pink letters of 'unsatisfactory progress' in front of her classmates … and she wasn't the only one. Apparently, it was the norm in this school district and pushed students to get higher grades. Really? At what cost?

With weekly testing, homework that often took over two hours to complete and absolutely no creativity in the curriculum, it quite frankly felt like child abuse. As an artist, I was passionate about bringing more creativity into the classroom, but I was only allowed to volunteer and teach art for one hour every two weeks. This was pretty much the children's only creative outlet at school.

Socially Gracie was fine – she had made new friends – but from a learning perspective my little girl's confidence was being crushed. I knew I had to do something about it and fast – time was of the essence.

One evening I had been watching a programme on Gaia (a Netflix for spiritual seekers) and it spoke of the 'Goddess Sophia'. My ears instantly pricked up as this was the first time I had ever heard of the Goddess Sophia and it sparked an innate curiosity. The next morning I woke up at 6am to continue reading my enthralling new book 'Mary Magdalene Revealed' by Meggan Watterson. As I opened the book midway through, and started to read, I couldn't believe it, as there in black and white was more information about the Goddess Sophia! Now, I don't know about you, but when something I have never heard of in my whole entire life comes up twice in the space of eight hours, I'm pretty sure that is no coincidence, but a divine synchronicity sent from the Universe to get my attention … it definitely had my attention!

That morning I took Gracie into my Reiki studio. We had been doing regular morning meditations to try to relieve her stress and anxiety about going to school. Gracie's third-grade teacher had told me that she had 'major focus issues' and recommended I put her on medication – shocking, I know. He also suggested that I have her 'psychologically assessed' as there was definitely something 'not quite right'. This unbelievable advice went against every part of my being and I knew that everything about it was wrong, but, still, it played on my fears and part of me began to worry that maybe there was something wrong.

As Gracie sat on my healing table with her eyes closed, she listened to the calming meditation music and breathed deeply. I stood behind my little girl and held my hands up in despair, as tears rolled down my cheeks. I silently cried out to the Divine Mother for the first time and asked with all of my being:

> *'Goddess Sophia, please help my little girl. Please send*
> *a solution to this problem. Please help us!'*

I lowered my hands to my heart and gave thanks before wiping my tears away and smiling for Gracie. 'OK my darling, let's get you to school.'

Just then I had a spontaneous idea … and one that was completely illogical. I decided that we should all take Gracie to school that morning at 7.45am, and then my husband (who had just flown in from Memphis the night before) and our three-year-old son, Lennon, would head to our local cafe for a morning coffee. Although it seemed like a great idea, it meant we had 20 minutes to get Lennon fed, dressed, shoes on and out of the door … The fact that we did this was a miracle in itself!

Sure enough we dropped Gracie at school on time and headed to the cafe. As we entered, I caught the gaze of a stranger looking at me with the most lovely, warm smile. I smiled back thinking 'Uh oh, I must know this woman, but I have no idea who she is.'

As we sat with our coffee and Lennon with his cake pop, my husband asked me, 'Who was that lady you were smiling at?' to which I replied, 'I've no idea, but the way she smiled at me was like she knew me.'

As we finished up our morning coconut lattes, we exited the coffee shop and I instinctively held the door just in case there was anyone following behind me. As I glanced back, there she was, the smiling stranger, but this time she had a little boy next to her who looked to be the same age as my son. The boys started playing and talking to each other in the small outdoor courtyard, which prompted the awkward, obligatory mum conversation …

Me: 'How old is your little boy?'

Mystery mum: 'He's just turned three.'

Me: 'Ahh my son is three, too!'

Mystery mum: 'I also have a nine-year-old.'

Me: 'Oh wow, I have a nine-year-old too!' (six years isn't a common age gap).

Mystery mum: 'My son goes to the neighbourhood school, but he is really struggling there. I have an interview at a new school tomorrow.'
Me (jaw agape): 'Oh wow, this is crazy. My daughter is at the same school and really struggling too.'

The conversation that followed was nothing short of miraculous. We had both been going through the exact same thing and had the same opinions with regards to the school district and the mainstream public school system. We joyfully hugged and swapped numbers as we said goodbye, relieved that we had found each other and we were not alone. As I hopped into the car I looked at my husband in disbelief, who in return looked back at me in disbelief.

'You have to write down what just happened because that was mind-blowing,' he said.

'Yeah, but do you know what is even more mind-blowing? I called on the Goddess Sophia for the first time ever this morning and then this happened!'

A couple of minutes later, my phone binged. It was a message from mystery mum, Nicole: 'Hey, loved meeting you this morning! I want to tell you there is a great school on Mulholland that has a space available in the fourth grade.'

I had never heard of the school, so I curiously went online and checked it out. It looked amazing but there were only 21 kids per year and apparently the school was notoriously hard to get in to. I called the school right away.

Me: 'Hi there, my name is Katy Sloane, I have a nine-year-old daughter who has just started fourth grade in Los Angeles Unified School District. We urgently need to switch her to a new school. Do you have any space?'

The woman paused and then stuttered as though lost for words, 'You are not going to believe this, but there is only one space available right now in the entire school and that is in fourth grade … for a girl!'

And there we have it, I thought, the final miracle of the morning from Sophia. My prayer had not only been answered, but it had been answered at pretty much the speed of light … okay maybe not quite but, seriously, this all transpired three hours after asking the Goddess Sophia for help!

We went to view the school and took a tour around the campus which was nothing short of amazing, all of the staff were so kind and caring. The school had a great vibe and the beautiful art and theatre building was the icing on the cake, creativity was valued and celebrated at this school. It was a perfect fit for Gracie.

In the week that followed there was a lot of paperwork, parent interviews and a few minor obstacles to overcome in order to get Gracie her place at the new school, but I knew that I need not worry for it was already done. The main hurdle was Gracie's old school teacher, who needed to write a letter of recommendation. 'Oh dear', I thought.

Logically I knew that this could prevent her getting the place, but intuitively I knew Sophia had it all in order.

Miraculously the school never received the teacher's 'recommendation' … or lack of it. Even though he had mailed it and then emailed it three times over! Sophia clearly had it all under control – after all, what was the zapping of a few emails in the ethers and the interception of an envelope to the Cosmic Mother of all that is? Ha! 'Piece of cake,' I thought, highly amused by the great effort her previous teacher had gone to make sure his voice was heard … sorry not sorry … keep your low vibes to yourself, mister!

Instead, the new school graciously decided to accept the glowing recommendation of Ms Chang, Gracie's lovely second-grade teacher from her previous Santa Monica school. Shortly after, Gracie was offered a place, which we gratefully accepted. We did it!

As for the mystery mum, Nicole, I messaged her a few times afterwards, but I never heard anything back. I often wonder whether she was, in fact, an angel sent to me that day in human form.

My first parents evening at the new school ended in tears when the teacher told me, 'Gracie is a joy to have, she has fit right in, she is so focused, she is often first to put her hand up in class and is such a happy child. We are so grateful to have her in our school. Do you have any questions for us Mrs Sloane?'

And all without medication … I was lost for words. If I'm honest, I had expected the teacher to tell me she had some concerns about focus at the very least.

Speechless, I eventually attempted to string a sentence together:
'Yes, so just to clarify … Do you have any concerns whatsoever?
About focus or … is there anything at all that you are concerned about?'

'No absolutely not, Mrs Sloane, Gracie is amazing!'

As my eyes welled up with tears of joy, I replied, 'Yes, yes she is!'

You see the miracles just kept on flowing because the power of the
Divine Mother is second to none.

After the flurry of divine synchronicities that transpired that beautiful
morning, I decided I wanted to learn everything I could about Sophia.
I ordered a beautiful book, which I found online, called 'Pistis Sophia'
by JJ Hurtak (not an easy read, but it does contain a bible of information
on the Divine Goddess). When it arrived, I opened the box with excited
anticipation and carefully took out a stunning, white, feminine-style bible
with a striking gold sacred geometric form on the front of it.

I gasped in utter disbelief, for as I looked at the image before me I couldn't
believe my eyes … I had already seen this image because I had created it
almost exactly a year and a half previous. This was one of my favourite
artworks, which represented the Source of the Universe, the major
archangels, and the perfect balance of divine feminine and masculine
energy. I laughed in amazement as, little did I know, the Divine Mother
had been speaking to me through my artwork all this time!

Metatron's Cube Artwork: Containing every conceivable shape that exists within the universe. The circles represent the feminine and the straight lines represent the masculine. The outer golden sphere represents the Source of creation.

After the mystical events of that beautiful morning, I made a promise to the Goddess Sophia that I would spread the word of her light and not be afraid to speak my truth.

And so it is.

Invocation for the Goddess Sophia

Take a moment to close your eyes and go inward. Take a nice deep breath and say this invocation:

> *'Goddess Sophia, please be with me and allow me to awaken to your wisdom and light. I am ready to learn more and activate the Goddess within, igniting the sacred fire of my soul. Thank you.'*

My quest for knowledge that ensued after these mind-blowing events led me to discover many more hidden truths about the Goddess Sophia. I had been guided on this path of discovery through my connection with Yeshua and I was excited to dive even deeper into the secret knowledge and wisdom of the Great Mother.

So, let me share with you a little of what I have learned about Sophia since the unfolding of these events.

Sophia is found throughout many of the ancient texts and scriptures and is known as Wisdom Incarnate, the Goddess of all those who are wise. There are many references to her in 'The Book of Proverbs, The Apocryphal (secret) Books of Sirach and The Wisdom of Solomon' written by Alexandrian Jews in the Hellenistic era.

In the latter text, the creation story is told using the word 'She'. The author praises her in her own right as 'holy' and 'all-powerful':

'Although she is but one, she can do all things,
and while remaining in herself, she renews all things;
in every generation she passes into holy souls and
makes them friends of God, and prophets; for God loves
nothing so much as the person who lives with wisdom.

She is more beautiful than the sun, and excels every
constellation of the stars.

Compared with the light she is found to be superior.'

Wisdom 7:27-29

Another interesting source of information regarding Sophia is in
The Pistis Sophia, which loosely translates to 'the faith of Sophia'. This is
a third-century text discovered in 1773 in which the risen Jesus Christ has
interactions with his closest disciples. Within these meetings, Jesus shares his
teachings of the Divine Mother and his experiences with her as he ascended
through the different dimensions and levels of consciousness after the
resurrection. These sacred texts contain dialogues between Jesus and Mary
Magdalene, his mother Mary, Martha of Bethany, and other disciples.

In this text Jesus explains who Sophia is when he says:

'Son of Man consented with Sophia, his consort, and
revealed a great androgynous light. Its male name is
designated "Saviour, begetter of all things". Its female
name is designated, "All begettress Sophia. Some call her
"Pistis".'

Although this seems somewhat cryptic and is open to interpretation, one thing we can be sure of is that Jesus clearly states there is a male and female aspect of God. When we look at how the world has functioned over the past few thousand years, with the domination of the masculine and the oppression of the feminine, it is no surprise that humanity and Earth are in such a dire state. To restore balance to the Earth, the feminine must rise up and the masculine must honour and respect her as his equal and sacred counterpart.

The Myth of the Goddess Sophia

In the Gnostic myth of how the world came to be, the feminine aspect of God that is Sophia, lives happily united with her divine masculine counterpart in the limitless potential of Source energy. Sophia becomes so distracted with love for the creative Source that when she sees a brilliant shimmering light below, she immediately descends into the darkness to greet it, following what she believes to be the creative divine light, but she soon realises she has been tricked by the false light. There, in the dark and unrealised potential of the world, she is separated from the true light and unable to ascend back to Source.

In these lower dimensions the rulers and energies of the underworld abuse and exploit her, until all she knows is sadness and despair in her arduous quest to return home to the original Source light. Trapped in the lower realms she gives birth to a mixed bag of demigods called archons who are blinded by the false light and obsessed with power and control.

The worst of this offspring is the demiurge who bring chaos and destruction, contaminating the world with pride, ignorance, fear, and an obsession for power and pleasure. However, Sophia counteracts these low vibrations by bringing great beauty and spiritual potential to the Earth and conceals divine light and consciousness in the body of the demiurge's first man, Adam, and then brings her light into the world as Eve.

Finally, Sophia breaks free from the chains of the lower dimensions and begins her ascent back up to the light of Source. Through her journey she raises the consciousness of humanity just a little, and through her love and empathy for humans she refuses to abandon them, knowing the depth of their pain and suffering. For this reason she fractures her consciousness, leaving part of herself behind in order to guide humans to awaken to their own divinity, and walk the path to enlightenment.

In the higher celestial realms, Sophia transcends into the pure and blissful light of Source through the reunification with her divine masculine counterpart.

Through this journey of pain and suffering Sophia is made ever more powerful through the growth of her experiences and this power is added to the androgynous whole. Sophia is now complete, full with the knowledge and wisdom of the transcendent, unified light.

In her book 'Return of the Divine Sophia,' Tricia McCannon states: 'The Gnostics believed that the origin of everything rests firmly in a Supreme First Principle – a secret, hidden, female Divinity –nameless, unknown, and unknowable and only silence can express this original Nothingness.'

Across that endless Cosmic Ocean arose a ripple that revealed the Divine Self. This Divine Self brought into existence a complex and highly paradoxical state of descending hierarchies, each with its own level of spiritual awareness. The highest state of being is manifested in the divine attributes of love, power, thought, compassion, mercy, truth, grace, silence, humanity and the Goddess Sophia.'

These ancient texts describe Sophia as not only the feminine aspect of the Creator, but also as a frequency that births and gives life to all that is.

Meditation and Invocation for Sophia

- Take a moment to close your eyes and go inward.

- Take a nice deep breath and say this invocation:

> '*I call upon the Goddess Sophia. May your golden light flow through every cell of my being, igniting the divine feminine wisdom within, and activating my own sovereignty as I remember the truth of who I really am. Thank you.*'

- As you take a deep breath in, imagine you are lying in a beautiful rose garden surrounded by trees. You lie on the soft grass and breathe in the sweet fragrance of the flowers. As you look up to the beautiful sky where the sun is setting, you see an array of fiery golden hues painted across the sky.

- A beautiful white dove comes into view. Soaring across the sunset sky, it swoops down towards you entering into the sacred rose garden and hovering above your chest.

- The dove transforms into a brilliant golden flame burning fervently above your heart.

- This is the cosmic flame of Sophia. As you stare into this cosmic flame, you see the spiralling light codes of creation, and sacred geometric patterns within it.

- The golden flame now melts into your heart chakra, activating a great fiery light within you.

- Feel the sacred flame of Sophia radiate out from your heart centre throughout your entire being.

- Feel it flowing up into your brain, illuminating your pineal gland as it expands with golden light.

- Feel the light balancing the left and right sides of your brain as the masculine and feminine energies are united.

- Now becoming aware of yourself as an orb of pure conscious light. Take this light from the haven of your mind and place it into your heart.

- Feel your conscious awareness connect into the portal of your heart and visualise your physical heart beating and glowing with the golden flame of Sophia.

- As you look into your heart, the golden light starts to swirl creating a powerful vortex, activating the sacred portal of your heart.

- Take your consciousness into this vortex, which transports you deep into the Earth where a beautiful silver white light appears. You pass through this light and are now in the sacred space of Gaia within the centre of the Earth.

- A magnificent Goddess appears before you, draped in a shimmering golden garment of light.

- She embraces you, enveloping you in her arms and you feel the power of her pure maternal love for you.

- She then creates a beautiful golden pink rose, filled with golden starlight and the wisdom of Sophia.

- She places this cosmic rose directly into your heart and says one word: 'Bloom'.

- Feeling a powerful surge of light manifest through this cosmic rose activation, you are lifted back up the vortex of light to the surface of Earth. This is where you must bloom and share your wisdom and light.

- As your consciousness unites with your physical body, you feel the power of the golden light of Sophia within you and in this moment you know that you are awakening to your unlimited potential.

- It is time for you to bloom. It is time for you to step into your true power and remember the flame of Sophia within.

- Take a moment of gratitude for this powerful activation and for the wisdom you have received.

Listen to this meditation at **katysloane.com/CGR**

The Hand of the Father: A Journey Beyond the Worlds of Matter

On 4 July 2021, I travelled to London to embark on a six-hour shamanic meditation experience with my lovely friend Lucy. At the beginning of the ceremony, we were guided to pull a card from a deck of angel cards. The healer facilitating the session told us that often the card you draw acts as an anchor throughout the shamanic journey. 'Interesting, I wonder what mine will be,' I thought. As I turned over my card, there was a picture of a divine masculine being with long white hair. The title above this picture read 'Father Sky.' Wow, this was so aligned as my intention for the ceremony was directly related to the divine masculine.

You see I had been on such a powerful quest with the divine feminine over the previous two years that I had felt quite disconnected to the divine masculine. I had also been receiving repeated reminders of the visitation I'd had as a child (see page 11); this apparition was, of course, a divine masculine being. I had therefore decided a few days prior that my intention for the journey was to discover more about the divine masculine aspect of the Creator. When I drew this card, I was amazed and gasped with excitement ... you know how I love a divine synchronicity! I then proceeded to explain to Lucy and the healers in the room why this card was so relevant.

With clear intentions, we ingested our plant medicine and laid back to receive higher guidance. At first the journey felt blissful – I saw images of sacred geometry flowing into my mind's eye and then a great golden hand appeared dipping below clouds in the sky. I knew without a doubt that this was the hand of the Father.

As I observed this magnificent vision, I heard Him say, 'My hand is right here for you. You can reach for it at any time.'

I was not prepared for what would happen next … instead of travelling to a realm of angels and fairies (like I had hoped), I descended into the underworld to face my darkest fears. Yup, not what I had in mind, but hey we can't dictate the lessons we need to learn, right? A loud, mechanical whirring noise reverberated through my head on repeat, over and over, as nauseating clanging sounds ricocheted through my skull. The colours coming through to my third eye were dark and muddied; there was nothing vibrant or magical about this place. It felt electrical, scattered, incoherent – oh and there were grim skull-faced hooded figures stood looking seriously creepy.

Thankfully, I remembered as I made my descent that I had the tools to get through this. I became aware that this was a gruelling initiation, so instead of running from the frightful scenes playing out before me, I was told to observe without judgement. 'Of course,' I thought, 'Remember what you teach and take a neutral perspective. This is just consciousness playing a role.' After what seemed like hours in this unpleasant lower realm, my mantra finally kicked in:

'Thank you for the lessons. Now take me to the light.'

I knew that I was not of this place, but I also knew it was important for me to see it. I had spent my whole life afraid of the dark and avoiding anything that might attract darkness. Here I was being made to face it and, instead of fearing it, I knew that my greatest weapon was to shine my light into this dark realm, for darkness is merely the absence of light.

'Thank you for the lessons. Now take me to the light. Thank you for the lessons. Now take me to the light,' I said over and over in my head. However, there was still more for me to learn in this lower realm. I started to see scenes from my life playing out before me – there were traumatic scenes, scenes of abuse and scenes where I was not all too proud of my behaviour. 'I'm sorry, I'm so sorry' I said, 'Why are you sorry?' a voice said. 'If you are sorry, you are judging yourself.'

I was made to watch the disturbing scenes again and again, until I stopped saying sorry and accepted the lessons, and in that moment I realised I was no longer judging myself for things that had happened in my past. I was accepting the experiences for the lessons and growth that they had brought. In this moment I realised that we are each our own judge and forgiveness of self is the key to our own inner peace.

Once I reached this place of compassion and acceptance for myself, the loud mechanical whirring began to fade and I remembered the message at the very beginning of the journey: 'My hand is right here for you. You can reach for it at any time.'

In this moment, I reached for His hand and I was instantly lifted out of the lower realms as I soared up into the light, feeling sheer relief at no longer hearing those gruelling sounds. As my consciousness was catapulted into the ethers, I found myself sat between the worlds of matter and the higher heavens. I sat in this blissful place looking down upon the Earth and in this moment everything made complete sense.

I was shown a low vibrational energetic grid all around the planet, it looked electrical and felt in resonance with the dark frequencies of the underworld. 'False gods, the false gods,' I thought. Sounds crazy, I know … I was being shown that the false gods had built this electrical energy grid around our planet in order to keep humanity in lower states of consciousness. Wait, who are the false gods? (Well there's no end to that rabbit hole but I'll touch upon it briefly a little later.) These harsh frequencies create disharmony and disease within the body and minds of humanity. This was some seriously deep stuff, but from my higher perspective everything made complete sense. When I think about it logically this grid could be many things. Think of the number of artificial signals that are relentlessly beamed across the planet - WiFi signals, cell phone towers, radio and television frequencies, and don't get me started on 5G radiation and the devastating effects we are beginning to see in relation to that. I believe the grid that I saw in my vision encompassed all these things, but artificial intelligence was the dominating vibration.

It was alarming to see the power that this energy held and it was clear that the vast majority of humans on the planet were in resonance with it. However, I knew from this higher state of awareness that I could navigate the Earth plane and detach from this destructive energy. I knew that my mission was to radiate a different frequency and help people to see there is another way of being.

The false gods are service-to-self beings who invisibly pull the strings to control the masses. Their main tool is to create as much fear as possible because whilst we are in fear we are easily controlled and remain enslaved to their self-serving system.

The good news is that their reign is coming to an end. There is a mass awakening happening on planet Earth. It has been prophesied for aeons and the darkness is screaming right now, as it desperately tries to stop the masses from awakening to their true power, to the great light within. Once we awaken to the truth, we are no longer enslaved to their systems of control.

Awaken dear friend, it is time.

As I peered upon the worlds of matter, I was given a greater understanding of everything. God the Father holds the construct of all that is. He is always there at the very core of creation and whenever we need Him we can reach for His hand. God the Mother is the creative force. She has descended into the lower dimensions with us. She experiences all of our pain and suffering and refuses to leave us until we awaken to the truth of who we are and ascend back home to be reunited with the Father/ Mother God, the Source of all that is. Deep, I know, but what an incredible journey and initiation!

Another miracle unfolded shortly after my journey. After sharing my experience about my trip to the underworld and the seeing the hand of God, with my friend Lucy, we left the space and made our way home. Over the next few days, I took time to journal as I integrated the incredible downloads of information that seemed like a thousand years' worth of knowledge and wisdom all in the space of a few hours. How could I possibly put into words all that I had witnessed and experienced that day? I did my best by sketching and writing as much as I could translate into the limited language of this third dimension. In particular, I drew the hand of God amongst the clouds and sketched other visions I had received.

Then something amazing happened. I received a message from a dear friend I had not heard from in over three years. She was checking in to see how I was doing and we got talking. She shared her perspective on everything going on in the world, amidst the pandemic, and said she hoped I didn't mind her being so open, to which I said 'Of course not, please feel free to share anything you feel guided to share with me.' The next message I received blew me away. This is what she wrote: 'There's a lady called Kat Kerr, who is a seer. I think you will love hearing about her visions. She just had a vision on the 4th of July, where she saw God's hand in the sky.'

WOW!!! Let's just take that in a moment. So not only did I also have a profound vision of God's hand in the sky, but my vision was also on the very same day, independence day … the 4th of July! I texted Lucy right away to tell her what had happened. Our minds were officially blown!

My experience that day brought me many lessons and so much growth and understanding of the higher and lower dimensions, but the most important thing was being able to observe myself and seeing that the pendulum in my mind was swinging too far the other way. My discovery of the buried truths of the Goddess had sparked an underlying resentment towards the masculine. It is easy to point the finger and blame men for the oppression of the feminine but the truth is that men have also been lied to and the void of the Divine Mother has cost them greatly also.

The Weakening of the Masculine

The suppression of the divine feminine has not only diminished women, but has weakened men by placing destructive expectations upon them to shut down their emotions and conform to a stoic, wounded warrior archetype. How many times have you heard or used the expression 'Man up'?

Men have been raised to suffer in silence and taught that to show their emotions is weak, causing them to suppress their pain and emotional trauma. This has led to great mental imbalance amongst men, with many seeing suicide as their only way out. Did you know that men make up an average of around 70 per cent of all suicides worldwide? The lost wisdom of the Great Mother has had a devastating effect on each and every one of us, both male and female.

It is so important for us to remember that gender is merely an expression of our physical vessels, but the soul is a perfect balance of each, just like the creator.

This simple equation of balance and unity can be applied to all areas of life. Let's look at the world of politics – we have the left and the right. These two seemingly opposing forces are constantly pitted against each other, each with the goal of destroying the other. You may be reading this now and identifying with your 'side', and that's okay but let me pose this question to you: wouldn't it be an extremely dull world if there was only one way of doing things? One of our greatest challenges at Earth school is to master polarity. In the ancient Hermetic teachings there are 7 key principles, one of which is 'The Principle of Polarity'.

In the book 'The Kybalion & The Emerald Tablet Of Hermes' it states,

'Everything is Dual; everything has poles; everything has its pair of opposites; like and unlike are the same; opposites are identical in nature, but different in degree; extremes meet; all truths are but half-truths; all paradoxes may be reconciled."

After studying these powerful ancient teachings I am naturally more mindful around triggering situations. I allow the feeling of frustration, anger, sadness (whatever it may be) to pass through me, breathing deeply before taking a step back and looking at things from a neutral point of view. This allows me to completely detach from drama and see things from a higher perspective.

I want you to really challenge yourself now. Think of a situation that has really triggered you. Can you look at both sides of the coin and see that there is truth in both? Can you step out of the 'I am right and you are wrong, box?'

Remember the ancient Hermetic teachings states that there is 50 per cent truth in everything. This is a real mind-bender, I know … a bit like the whole 'time is an illusion' thing, but the more you open your mind to this concept, the more you will begin to see that there is always truth on both sides and neither side is superior to the other. It doesn't have to be a constant battle; everything just is and that's okay! Although you may never agree with certain views or opinions, you will begin to accept that there is an element of truth in every perspective and instead of rejecting and setting out to destroy something because it doesn't conform to our way of thinking, we can accept that everything has its place and adds to the many levels of consciousness forever expanding and playing out on the great stage that is Earth.

When I think of the oppression of women and the dishonouring of the feminine I often wonder if on a karmic level things may once have been the other way around. Maybe there was once a time when women oppressed men and stripped them of their rights. If the universal law of karma is always at play then this has to be the case, right?

It was only when researching the Essenes that I began to believe that this absolutely was the case.

In the revelatory book, 'The Way of the Essenes: Christ's Hidden Life Remembered' there is a reference to Earth 8,000 years ago where women dominated men and treated them as slaves. It says:

> 'Woman oppressed man and man stifled his own
> cry.' It then goes on to describe the universal
> pendulum, 'swinging back and forth, from left to right.
> It is the law of justice and of forces tending toward
> equilibrium. It is the law of worlds ... the inbreath and
> outbreath of everything. This oppression will continue to
> pass from one to the other ... as long as men and women
> fail to understand that they are like the right and
> left hands of the man Kadmon' (the primordial man,
> linking God, man and the world).

In the ancient Hermetica 'The Principle of Rhythm' echoes this very sentiment, it says,

> *'Everything flows, out and in; everything has its tides;*
> *all things rise and fall; the pendulum-swing manifests in*
> *everything; the measure of the swing to the right is the*
> *measure of the swing to the left.'*

The Essenes believed that Yeshua came here to unite the masculine and the feminine, in 'The Way of the Essenes' it says: 'He will bear the face that speaks to the masculine soul, to the metal of its reason; and he will take on as well the face that speaks to the feminine soul, to the innermost recesses of its heart.'

I believe Yeshua came to Earth to tame the swing of the universal pendulum so that man and woman may meet in the middle and birth a new consciousness together. This is 'the middle path of enlightenment' that Yeshua so often spoke of.

As we go through this resurgence of the creative spirit of the Divine Mother, it is important to remember the Earth is coming back into a state of balance. It is not for the matriarch to overpower and dominate the patriarch, but rather for us to reach a state of equilibrium where the Earth and all living beings can flourish and live in peace and harmony in a higher vibration (the fifth dimension). On the macro, the formidable energy of the Divine Mother is rising from the ashes and restoring balance to the planet. On the micro, the hearts and minds of humanity are evolving, bringing a higher awareness as the brain shifts from the domination of left-brain logical thinking to balance with right-brain intuitive thinking.

When the masculine and feminine energies unite and balance is restored within us, we are able to access our multi-dimensional selves, opening the door to other worlds and realities beyond our wildest dreams!

It is time for us all to rise up and remember our own divinity.

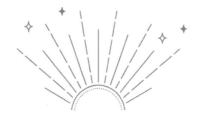

PART THREE

RISING

PART THREE:

RISING

The divine feminine is rising, lost truths are rising, our consciousness is rising, Gaia and the vibration of the planet is rising, this is truly a monumental time to be alive in the history of Earth, in the history of the Universe! I ask you this question: do you want to rise into the next phase of conscious evolution? If the answer is yes (cos, erm, why wouldn't it be?), then now is the time to channel your energy into raising your vibration so that you can rise with Gaia. We have a choice, and there is no right or wrong, but for those of us that choose the path of ascension, a beautiful world awaits. The New Earth is dawning and the Goddess, celestial beings, and Gaia herself, will be our greatest guides as we shift into the fifth dimension.

Allow this section of the book to aid you in raising your vibration to such a level that you soar into the New Earth. Remember, everything is energy and lower vibrations will not be compatible with this new way of being, so let's shed all that no longer serves us and bring on the high vibes!

3D TO 5D:

FEAR TO UNITY AND COSMIC CONSCIOUSNESS

The great shift from 3D to 5D is something that has been widely talked about by the great sages of the past and is a particularly hot topic of the present, as we are experiencing major changes on the Earth plane. It is something that has been well documented in the ancient texts and by many spiritual authors over the past century. Earth is in the process of shifting into a higher dimensional frequency. I am sure you have heard a lot of talk in the spiritual community about the shift from the third dimension to the fifth … But what happened to the fourth?

Well, the fourth dimension acts as a bridge to the fifth. It can be reached in the sleep state and includes the astral realm. Think of the fourth dimension as a form of training ground in between the third and the fifth. We spend around a third of our life in the fourth dimension while we are sleeping. It is a space where souls can learn and prepare for the different universal laws that apply in the higher dimensions. For instance, when you are in the astral realm, immersed in the fourth density, you have the ability to manifest things instantly through thought. Pretty cool, right? Well, yes … but only if you have disciplined your mind enough to think positively about the things you want. If you allow negative thoughts and fears to come through in the astral realm, you will instantly manifest those things and that can be pretty scary!

I believe that in our dream state we have been practising the art of conscious creation and learning great lessons to prepare for the great shift here on Earth.

Once you reach a certain vibration and level of understanding, you will begin to integrate the higher fourth and fifth dimensional frequencies into your physical body and you will start to notice accelerated manifestation in your waking state. You will find yourself thinking of something and then, almost instantly, it will be brought into your existence in some form. For example, recently it was a Full Moon and this particular Moon was called the Strawberry Moon. I wrote all about this Moon in my monthly newsletter and began to crave strawberries! I went to the shop and bought a punnet of big, juicy, red strawberries and myself and the kids devoured them after dinner that day. The next morning I woke up wishing there were still some strawberries left for breakfast. I then decided to clear out my coffee-maker and went into the garden to put the coffee grinds into the soil; only this time I bypassed the usual spot and walked to the back fence where I put the coffee grinds into the earth. As I did this, I noticed an old plant pot in the corner. I walked over to it and as I peered down into the pot, you will never believe what was in there … two strawberry plants, sporting little juicy red strawberries! I couldn't believe it. I didn't even know we had strawberry plants in the garden! I smiled to myself … 'Instant manifestation', I thought.

At first you may be a little freaked out by how quickly things pop into your reality, but soon you will begin to see the bigger picture as you realise that everything is connected and your thoughts are powerful signals rebounding back to you the frequencies you put out. Over time, you will become aware that you are a conscious creator and begin to take control of your mind by becoming the observer of yourself and the powerful thought energy you are radiating out into the ever-responding cosmic field of consciousness.

As your vibration continues to rise, you will likely notice changes in your diet as you naturally gravitate towards lighter foods, weaning off meats and processed junk foods.

If we are to raise our vibration to fifth-dimensional levels, we must begin to detox our physical bodies, which will eventually become less dense as we integrate the higher frequencies. Sounds cuckoo I know but trust me, we have been in a box of logical thinking for so long that it is difficult to comprehend such things could actually be happening. My perception of reality has shifted so dramatically over the past decade that sometimes I catch myself wondering if I'm in some kind of crazy sci-fi movie. I think many of us can relate to this, especially as we entered into the twilight zone of 2020 with all its madness. I ask you this question: a few years ago would you ever have dreamed that what has transpired globally over the past few years could actually be real? Yet it happened and, as unbelievable as we would have previously thought it, here we are living through it!

So, hang on in there light tribe because glorious times are ahead …
New Earth awaits. We just have to ride the waves to get there.

Dolores Cannon's books bring extensive information on the New Earth and the great shift into the fifth dimension. Dolores developed her own method for regressing her clients and accessing valuable information from past lives and interdimensional beings. In her book 'The Three Waves of Volunteers and the New Earth,' she questions a regressed individual about the New Earth. The subject says:

> *'It's a big time on your planet … This is where you, as a planet, awaken out of the dream of thinking you are alone … All eyes are on Earth right now … Even children that come in, even for hours. You'll all carry that, the badge of having been here …*

No planet has ever quite evolved in this way before …
If you were going to have the option to carry the
identification of having been on a planet that will be
known through the multiverse, even if you can be here for
a few hours, that you could say, "I was on Earth at the
time of evolution." Why not?'

This is truly such an exciting time to be alive; those of us that are here on Earth right now took on an incredible mission. We chose to be here for the great shift in consciousness, we chose to wade through the heaviness as the third-dimensional systems crumble, and bear witness to the dawning of a new era of love, peace and cosmic connection.

I pose an important question to you: what if this time of division and chaos before the great shift is actually one great initiation? A test for humanity? The ancient Egyptian mystery schools used to put their students through gruelling initiations in order to learn the lessons needed to attain enlightenment. Collectively we were made to face our greatest fears through the pandemic … the fear of death. If we as a society were not so afraid of death, we would deal with things very differently. Ironically fear is the biggest stressor to your immune system.

In his book 'The Biology of Belief,' Dr Bruce Lipton states, 'Being in a fear mindset will activate your HPA axis, because of that the body will go into fight or flight response, forcing blood into the extremities in order to survive against the perceived external threat and away from the viscera (gut), lowering the immune system and putting us at high risk of dis-ease.'

In other words, simply put, fear will make you sick. Being in the vibration of fear will also close you off from your higher self, steering you into left-brain logical thinking with no access to your intuition. The powers that be know this all too well, which is why they unleashed the biggest campaign of fear throughout the whole Covid-19 pandemic, with daily death counts emblazoned across the TV.

If you haven't already, please stop watching the news. Everything is vibration ... *'I feel amazing after watching the news'* said no one ever. It's time to start becoming aware of the external frequencies you are exposing yourself to. Ask yourself, does this make me feel good? If the answer is no, then remove yourself from that energy or vice versa. It's time to smash the old records of fear and programming and start thinking for ourselves as sovereign beings. As we integrate the fifth-dimensional frequencies of the New Earth, we begin to see through the illusions of this reality. As the veil of amnesia is lifted, we remember who we are and where we came from. We are multi-dimensional beings of light who volunteered to enter into a physical vessel to help anchor light onto this planet and save humanity from its own destruction.

At the end of the day, we always have two choices: we either choose to be governed by fear or we choose to be governed by love. Love or fear, everything comes down to these two vibrations. The one you choose will determine your soul's path.

Choose love.

A Visitation From the Stars

Let me take you back to mid-December 2013. I was living in Santa Monica in a lovely house, 14 blocks from the ocean. At this time in my life, I was feeling a little lost, like I was punching against the tide. I was also extremely worried about my sister Sarah, who was an alcoholic and going through a mental breakdown. Her drinking was out of control and had got to a point where it was dangerous for her to stop drinking completely; she would need to reduce her intake gradually to avoid fitting and seizures. I had been shown a very upsetting vision of my sister in a Reiki distance session I did for her, and this was when I knew things were really bad. In this vision, I was shown a future where my sister was no longer with us on the Earth plane; she had passed, leaving her husband and two children to navigate life without her. This was extremely distressing to see. I was being shown that this was the timeline that my sister was currently on and if something didn't change soon we would lose her. I had tried to warn the family back in England that things were a lot worse than they seemed, but my sister definitely put on a great act of pretending she was okay. I had told the family about my vision, but to be honest I think they thought I was being crazy. Cut to 2016 and my sister is on life support after having had yet another seizure; the doctors have given her a 50/50 chance of pulling through. We are all beyond devastated.

Let me backtrack a little: one evening in December 2013 I was chopping cucumber in the kitchen, deep in thought about my sister and the disturbing vision I had been given about her. I felt the emotion building within me. I felt completely powerless, knowing that only she could turn this around; it was like a volcano of emotion stirring within me just waiting to erupt. Suddenly the knife missed the cucumber, slicing my finger badly. Ouch! I gasped in pain, running to the kitchen sink to place it under the cold running water before wrapping it tightly in kitchen roll.

The volcano then erupted. I hurried to the bedroom and quickly closed the door. Throwing myself onto my bed, I wept uncontrollably with my face planted directly into the pillow. I cried like I had never cried before, as all the energy and emotions that had built up over that year were released in this moment.

I then became aware of a powerful energy building around me. It was so strong that in the midst of my sobbing, I slowly lifted my head from the pillow to see where it was coming from. The room looked like a mirage, as waves of invisible energy flowed towards me and there in the corner of the room, around 10 feet away, was an incredible blue interdimensional being of light. I instantly locked eyes with this cosmic being for what seemed like an eternity, although in reality it was probably more like 20 seconds.

I was completely mesmerised by the loving vibration of this beautiful being from the stars. My eyes locked into its big almond-shaped inky-black eyes, which carried so much depth they felt as though the entire Universe was contained within them. So much love was emanating from this being of pure light; it looked very alien-like, but it did not have a dense physical body and it radiated a very feminine, maternal vibration. I knew I was deeply connected to this being, but I had no idea what it was or from where it came.

If the fear narrative that has been played in the media on repeat for decades around extraterrestrials was anything to go by, then I should have been scared out of my mind, but in reality this being looked at me with such pure unconditional love that fear could not possibly come into the equation.

Its appearance was androgynous, but its loving energy felt very motherly, warm and nurturing; to me its vibration was distinctly female.

After this mesmerising moment, when time had literally stood still, the cosmic being faded into the ethers and, there I was, completely stunned on my bed looking at the corner of the bedroom in utter shock, awe and wonder.

I walked out to my husband who was in the living room watching TV and relayed to him what had just happened. I then proceeded to search the internet looking for anything that looked remotely similar to the being I had seen, but there was nothing that even came close.

I felt like I couldn't share my story with anyone apart from my husband for fear of ridicule, but I desperately wanted to know what this being was and why it had appeared to me. What was the message behind it? In April 2014 I thought I had found the answer. I drove from LA to San Francisco to meet a highly recommended mystic that can physically see angels and spirits. I felt sure that she would be able to tell me what the being was and what it all meant.

Unfortunately, I was taught a very abrupt lesson that day. After travelling all that way and having the courage to tell her my story, she told me that it was simply a hallucination.

My heart sank. I felt so hurt and disappointed as I knew what I had seen was very real and by no means a hallucination. For the next five years I put the experience to the back of my mind and buried my gnawing curiosity. I did not talk to anyone about it, nor did I research anymore into it. I was wounded by the experience with the psychic and I felt that if she of all people was doubting my experience, then so would everyone else.

Fast forward to 2019, my sister is alive and well after making a truly miraculous recovery and I am on a roll, discovering the lost teachings of Jesus and the ineffable power of the divine mother and the Goddess Sophia. I had officially got my mojo back and I was accessing levels of energy and information that empowered me beyond belief. Never again would I seek external validation from anyone – I had indeed become my own guru! Standing in my truth, I was ready to revisit the memory of this phenomenal experience again and seek the true meaning within it.

After the many miracles that had unfolded with Sophia, I decided it was time to find out why this strangely familiar star being had visited me that day and what it meant. I went to my Reiki studio and said an invocation to Sophia that went something like this:

> *'Sophia, please help me to find out what kind of being*
> *appeared to me that day and why it visited me.*
> *I am ready to learn and I know that you will guide me to*
> *find the answers. Thank you!'*

I left my Reiki studio feeling psyched to be back on the cosmic train of discovery. Suddenly the white bookcase in the corner of my living room grabbed my attention and I found myself automatically walking towards it. I scanned the shelf and intuitively picked out a book called 'The Book of Knowledge: The Keys of Enoch' by J. J. Hurtak. This was the sister book to the Pistis Sophia, another complex bible of mind-blowing metaphysical information. As I held the white, leather-bound book, I decided to open it on a random page. The pages buzzed like a humming bird as I flipped through a few hundred pages and then stopped. As I studied the seemingly random page, I read the title out loud 'The Shepherd Arcturus'.

Hmm, so strangely familiar was this name 'Arcturus'. I read on and learned that the shepherd Arcturus was actually a prophet, yet I had never heard of him. Who was he? I Googled his name, looking for clarity, confused as to why his name resonated with me so much. I couldn't find anything of any relevance on a general web search, so I decided to click 'images' on the tool bar. As I scrolled through several pages, I gasped as one particular image jumped out at me. I stared in utter disbelief, as there it was, an almost identical image of the being that had appeared to me!

I could not contain my excitement. As I dug deeper, I learned the being was an Arcturian from a star called Arcturus in the Boötes star constellation – collectively they are known as Arcturians! From this moment on, I wanted to learn everything I could about these amazing star beings. My husband and I searched the web looking for information and ordered several books on the Arcturians.

Once I began to learn more about these amazing beings, it all started to fall into place. You see, the Arcturians work very closely with the angelic realms; they are divine feminine heart-centred beings and are some of the most advanced beings in our Universe. They are assisting humanity and Earth with the ascension process as they are fifth-dimensional beings and have pure light bodies, just like angels! All the information confirmed so much of what I had intuitively felt during the visitation.

We have a lot to learn from our Arcturian friends, that is for sure!

As our hearts and minds expand, we are freed from the separation and fear of the third dimension, entering into Cosmic Consciousness where we are able to access higher states of awareness.

With this comes the ability to consciously connect with angels, light beings, loved ones passed and, last but not least, our brothers and sisters from the stars.

To learn more about my sister's miraculous recovery listen to 'The Ether Real Podcast', episode 1. You can also access this via my website katysloane.com

Angels of the Cosmos

My journey of discovery with the Arcturians has continued to grow and flourish. I love that these beautiful light beings work so closely with the angelic realms … of course they do! My journey with the angels continues to lead me to places I could never have even imagined possible. I know that they helped me to open this magical door to the stars, deepening my understanding and connection to the Cosmos and the angelic realms. Before my awakening to star beings, I had always thought of angels as only being assigned to help humans here on Earth, but now I realise there is an abundance of angels throughout all of creation. The Universe is overflowing with life and there are angels that guide many other life forms within this Universe and throughout the multiverse.

As we connect with the celestial realms, our awareness begins to shift out of logical linear thinking and separation consciousness, evolving into unity and Cosmic Consciousness. With this comes absolute knowing that the Universe is bustling with life.

As we explore Cosmic Consciousness, we are able to connect to other star races, many of which work in unison with the angelic realms and are helping Earth and humanity tremendously at this time. Such beings are of course the Arcturians, Pleiadians, Sirians and Lyrans, to name but a few.

The foundations of our reality are being shaken so that we may awaken and free our minds, shifting into the next stage of conscious evolution. We are in a time of accelerated growth and the only way to shift out of fear and into love is to release harsh judgements and start acting from the heart. Your heart is a portal; choose love and the path of ascension awaits.

Here is one of my favourite pieces of artwork inspired by the Arcturians and the many angels of the Cosmos helping Earth at this time. I love to raise the vibe of my home through creating my own celestial-inspired art; there is literally a piece of my artwork in every room, with each piece reminding me of our innate connection to the higher realms. Whether you class yourself as an artist or not, everyone can create their own masterpiece. Allowing yourself to let go and express yourself through art is so good for the soul and can help you to heal, release blocks and even manifest your dreams into reality!

Angel of the Cosmos Painting (next page): Honouring the Goddess, angelic realms, the Arcturians, Pleiadian, Andromedans, Sirians and all of the many other light beings helping Earth at this time. This piece is a great reminder that our entire Universe is bustling with life and if we open our hearts and minds we can shift into cosmic consciousness …the next phase of human evolution.

Energy Ritual: Your Life is a Canvas

Art is my number one technique to get my creative, intuitive juices flowing. Below is an exercise that will lift your vibe, shift creative blocks and help you to manifest a bright and beautiful future … and all through the power of painting.

You will need a large piece of paper or a large canvas – I recommend at least A2 size, which translates roughly to 17 x 24 inches. If you're feeling really artistic, use a large canvas instead of paper. I prefer canvas as it gives you the freedom to use lashings of paint!

Now divide your page/canvas into four sections. The first three sections will represent the three chapters of your life up to the present moment, the fourth section will represent the future. Don't get too hung up on where the first three sections begin and end; this is a right- brain intuition exercise, so listen to your inner guidance and you will know what each chapter of your life feels like. As you look over these segments, what emotions do you feel when you think about each one? I want you to close your eyes and really feel into each part … what memories can you find within each one?

Here is an example of my three chapters:

Chapter 1: Childhood

Chapter 2: Teenage into 20s

Chapter 3: The beginning of motherhood in my mid-20s to present day

Chapter 4: My future

As you focus on the first three chapters of your life and the memories within it, think about what colours best represent your experiences. Allow your inner child to surface and let your energy flow through the paintbrush onto the canvas. Remember there is no right or wrong in art; you can express yourself freely in this exercise without ever worrying about making a mistake. If you want to add words or symbols, go right ahead – this is your masterpiece.

Once you have filled the first three chapters with your chosen colours, take a step back and look at what you have created so far. Look at the array of colours representing the beautiful story of your life. Of course, there are challenges and traumas within every story, but that is what adds such depth. As you embark upon the fourth chapter of your painting, I want you to believe that the best is yet to come. Stand strong in front of your canvas and visualise your dreams becoming reality. There is so much light in your future – as you walk upon your spiritual path, there are many miracles and divine opportunities that flow to you. Feel gratitude in your heart as this fourth chapter radiates divine flow and synchronicity.

Once you have raised your vibration through feeling into the joy and fulfilment of the future, begin to channel this energy into your painting.

This is a powerful exercise not only for opening your creative, intuitive centres but for visualising a beautiful future for yourself and your loved ones as you step into the role of conscious creator.

CHAPTER 13

RAISING YOUR VIBE IN YOUR SACRED SPACE

Once you have created your life canvas, you can place it in your sacred space and when you look at it you will be reminded of how far you have come and the amazing things that are yet to come. Remember this is your place to connect to your angels and guides daily; a reminder to invite more light into your life. When you repeatedly connect to the light in one particular place, you gradually build up a positive residual energy within that space and, over time, you will begin to feel the frequency of the high-vibrational energy that you have created through consistent connection to the angelic realms.

In my Reiki and meditation studio, clients always comment on the beautiful energy of the room as soon as they step into it. This is because it is imbued with angelic frequencies and, over time, through repeated connection to the angels and the divine, a portal of light has been formed. So many profound experiences have taken place within my sacred spaces over the years ... I can't wait for you to create your own mini portal of light!

Reiki

Absolutely anyone can do Reiki; it is an amazing life tool to have. If you decide you would like to learn this healing art form, there are many ways to train. It is usually possible to gain your level one certification within a day or two and begin channelling the energy immediately. I offer several options for trainings and group certifications. For more information head to **katysloane.com/reiki**

Whether you decide to delve into the world of energy healing or not, everyone can benefit from learning the five Reiki principles:

Just for today I will not worry.
Just for today I will not be angry.
Just for today I will do my work honestly.
Just for today I will give thanks for my many blessings.
Just for today I will be kind to my neighbour
and every living thing.

Just reading these basic but powerful principles out loud will help you to stay centred and remind you to be present. The five Reiki principles work well for daily affirmations and can also be applied as mantras during meditation. Have a play and see what feels right for you. Simply reading them to yourself will lift your vibration.

Once you awaken to your inner healer, you will know that you can always channel this energy to heal yourself and others and empower your life across all areas.

Remember Reiki can be used for manifestation and all kinds of weird and wonderful things. Like meditation, it will be your superpower!

Meditation

Hopefully you have already experienced and enjoyed the powerful meditations within this book and are open to trying new ways to meditate. I spoke about meditation in the Introduction (see page 41) and how it is a workout for the mind. As with a physical workout, you have to find what you enjoy. Meditation is the same. There are different types that you can try to see what suits you. However, in its simplest form, meditation is connecting to the breath and calming the mind.

Here are some different kinds of meditation you might like to experiment with:

- Guided meditation

- Guided angel meditation

- Crystal meditation

- Transcendental Meditation (TM)

- Breathwork (check out Wim Hof and how to 'get high off your own supply!')

- Sound healing meditation

- Mantra meditations

So, needless to say, my favourite kind are guided angel meditations. I host these live every month as part of my 'Celestial Tribe Membership'. In these magical classes, I go live via Zoom across the globe and I just love thinking of all my amazing members as beacons of light dotted across the world, all anchoring celestial light onto the Earth plane!

I am so grateful to have this consistent connection with my fellow light warriors in this magical tribe. If you are craving more angelic connection then this is a powerful way to regularly connect to the angels through my guidance and unique channelled meditations. For more information, go to **katysloane.com/celestial-tribe**

My favourite meditation studio to teach at is, without a doubt, Unplug Meditation in Los Angeles. It is the first meditation-only studio in the world and hosts an array of amazing classes with an eclectic mix of incredible teachers, such as Camilla Sacre-Dallerup, Carolina Goldberg, Ben Decker and Davidji.

It's the crème de la crème of meditation studios and there are so many magical and metaphysical classes for you to explore there.

I first began teaching at Unplug back in 2019 when they hosted my 'Angels and Meditation' art exhibition, which was all thanks to my dear friend Camilla Sacre-Dallerup, who after seeing my artwork suggested I exhibit it at Unplug. As plans were put in motion for Unplug's first ever art exhibition, the owner, Suze Yalof Schwartz, suggested I conduct a live meditation alongside my artwork. I'm so glad she did as the response was amazing! So many people shared their profound angelic experiences after class, it was mind-blowing.

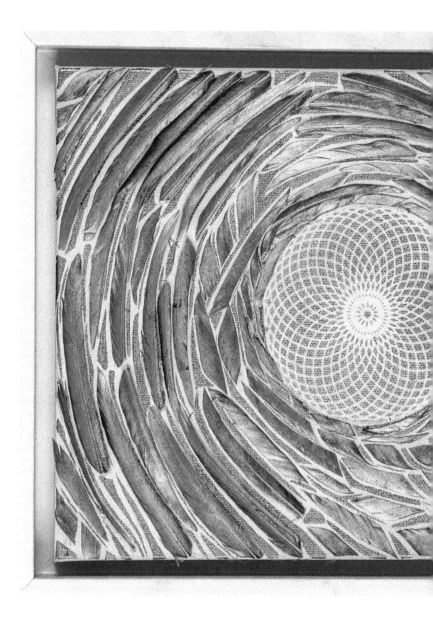

*Soul Star Vortex: We all have our
own energy vortex, which is constantly
spinning and attracting that which
we give thought to. Through meditation
we can clear the mind and centre our
energy in the vortex. When we align
in our vortex we can become the creator
of our reality and wonderful experiences
flow to us.*

*This piece is a powerful reminder
to stay centered in the vortex, and
create your best life.*

Since then, I have conducted regular guided angel meditations and workshops for Unplug and it has been amazing seeing so many people showing up to meditate with me and the angels. We have a full house every time and have even expanded into hybrid classes, so that no one gets turned away. People can now join online and experience the magic in the comfort of their own sacred space.

You know I'm big on having your own sacred space, but I want you to know that you can meditate anywhere. All you need to do is take a moment to connect to your breath and let the thoughts settle; this is meditation in its simplest form. If you can take just ten minutes every morning to breathe and connect to the light, you will set a strong foundation for the day ahead and everything will be in flow. Here are just a few benefits of meditation:

- Boosts the immune system
- Improves fertility
- Decreases stress
- Increases self-confidence
- Improves relationships
- Boosts creativity
- Reverses dis-ease
- Improves sleep
- Alleviates anxiety
- Lifts depression

- Lowers blood pressure

- Improves memory

- Regulates mood

- Helps with addiction

So, what are you waiting for? Get your medoface on and start radiating that attitude of gratitude!

Gratitude

One of my top hacks for lifting your vibe is to practise gratitude daily. A gratitude journal is a powerful tool to get you in the zone and align your energy for a smooth day ahead. Spending just five minutes a day writing a list of what you are grateful for will shift you into the vibration of gratitude and therefore create more things to be grateful for.

Recently, while driving in my car after a tumultuous school run, I found myself in a terrible mood. You know one of those mornings when you feel like a stuck record player? I must have asked my kids to put their shoes on ten times over, only to discover that my son had the wrong shoes on in the car on the way to school – those snazzy flashing Spider-Man sneakers sure stuck out like a sore thumb with his school uniform. Okay, I'm totally seeing the funny side now. A bit like when I did the most fabulous crazy hair day for my daughter (blue spray paint and all), only to drop her at school and realise no one else had crazy hair as it was not crazy hair day. Ahhh, mum life! Sorry, I totally digress.

So, I'm in a foul mood driving in the car on my way home after school drop-off, when I begin to observe myself. I know that this low-vibe mood I'm in is now my point of attraction. In other words, if I don't shift out of this bad mood, it's just going to get worse. The Universe will send me more things to be in a big fat mood about.

I instantly switched my focus to gratitude: 'Thank you, thank you, thank you for this car I am driving.' 'What else?' I thought as I looked out of the window and saw the beautiful trees lining the road.

'Thank you for the trees, thank you for the birds, thank you for the sunshine and clouds in the sky.' I was on a roll now. I started listing as many things as I could find to be grateful for. No matter how small, I said thank you for it. An involuntary smile started to manifest across my face and I became aware that I was no longer thinking about the awful morning that had just transpired, and then when it popped into my head I actually started laughing about the ridiculousness of the events that had unfolded. 'Jeez, stop taking life so seriously,' I thought to myself. Gratitude had uplifted my mood pretty much instantly … and boy was I grateful for that!

Practising gratitude is super-easy. It doesn't have to be for anything big; it can be for something as simple as the clothes you are wearing or the cup of coffee you are drinking. There is always so much to be grateful for. The more you practise living in the vibration of gratitude, the more the Universe will send you things to be grateful for. Keeping a daily gratitude journal is a quick way of shifting and lifting your vibe.

Visualisation

Visualisation is another powerful tool for raising your vibration and can be used to support you in your daily life, alongside manifesting your goals and desires. Taking a moment to visualise your day being in flow is a game-changer. Sometimes if I am feeling overwhelmed as I have too many things to do in one day I will stop, close my eyes and breathe, as I visualise everything flowing effortlessly in my day. I will really feel into the emotion as I visualise getting everything done and how good that feels. After holding the visualisation, I will then use an affirmation to empower it such as:

> *'This day is harmonious and everything is in flow.*
> *I achieve all I want to do and more.'*

This is super-simple to do and by taking just a few minutes out of your day to visualise a successful day, you will save yourself so much time and energy.

Visualisation is a key player in manifesting your dreams. There is a reason why the Navy SEALs use meditation and visualisation as a powerful tool for achieving success on their missions. My husband has first-hand experience of this after he trained at SEALFIT with Commander Mark Divine in Encinitas, California. You can hear all about his experience on my podcast, 'The Ether Real Podcast'. To say he was put through the ringer was an understatement, but his main takeaway was that mental strength is everything.

Believe you can do it and don't give up; visualise your own success! Mark Divine says: 'Visualisation is one of the most important concepts for people to learn and anchoring the correct feeling to the visual picture. When I personally train people to retrain the brain, I ensure that we not only create the picture or movie of what people want. I anchor the correct feeling to the picture and also create a strong mantra for them to read daily.'

I have done this many times with the creation of this book, visualising the physical copy in my hands and how good that will feel, seeing people reading my book and lighting up on the inside … eeek, I can feel the joy and excitement rising within me now!

'I am so grateful for my published book.'

Oh, how I love an affirmation!

Affirmations

Affirmations are positive statements that help us to overcome self-sabotaging and negative thoughts. When you repeat affirmations and begin to believe them, you rewire your brain and begin to attract the essence of the words. Here are some of my favourite affirmations that I often use in my daily life:

'I am love.'

'I am strong.'

'I am healthy.'

'I am joy.'

'Abundance flows to me.'

'I am supported and loved by the Universe.'

'I am surrounded and guided by angels.'

'I am exactly where I am supposed to be.'

'I am an infinite being of light.'

'All is well.'

'I am' is a powerful way to begin an affirmation as it represents the 'I am presence' which is the light of Source within you. So, every time you say 'I am ...' followed by something positive, you empower and uplift your energy. On the flip side, when you say 'I am' followed by something negative, you disempower your divine self.

Empower yourself and lift your vibe with positive 'I am' statements.

With affirmations, it is important to use the present tense as though it is happening right now in the present moment.

The Universe is always responding to your vibration, so if you are living in the past and thinking about negative experiences that have happened to you, you are putting out the same frequency and will therefore create more low-vibration experiences by default. This is why it is so important to live in the present moment; all we ever have is this moment right now.

Sometimes my students get hung up on their vibration not matching the affirmation; for instance, they may be feeling unwell and therefore the affirmation 'I am healthy' doesn't represent how they are actually feeling. I always tell them not to worry as this is the whole point. We want to change our vibration so that we feel healthy and the affirmation 'I am healthy' holds a vibration of health, which will positively impact our energy and subconscious mind. Keep saying it and hold a visualisation of health, soon enough you will be a picture of health!

Mantras

Mantras are sacred repetitive sound vibrations used to permeate the depths of the subconscious mind and heal imbalances within your energy field. You can work with mantras by chanting them out loud, listening to them from an external source, or by mentally vibrating a mantra in meditation. The power of a mantra is magnified by faith, intention and concentration.

In Buddhism, mantras are used to heal and transcend into higher states of consciousness. In Hinduism, the Sanskrit word 'Om' is considered to be the greatest of all the mantras, its sacred vibration is thought to be the sound of creation, expressing universal truth. As we explore the power of mantras we are reminded of the potency of our words.

It is important to observe our words and to become aware of how we talk to ourselves and others. We must be especially mindful of how we talk to ourselves. I always pose the question, 'Would you talk to your best friend the way you talk to yourself?' You are your own best friend; you have to take care of yourself first and foremost to be able to take care of and be there for other people. You are worthy and deserve to be treated with love, care and respect. Self-love is not selfish; it is essential for a healthy mind, body and spirit.

One of my favourite mantras to uplift, heal and create a harmonious relationship with myself and others is Ho'oponopono. This is a powerful ancient Hawaiian practice of forgiveness. It translates to:

'Thank you, I'm sorry, please forgive me, I love you.'

However, the meaning of this mantra runs far deeper and is believed to heal on many levels, erasing errors in thought and releasing destructive false beliefs within the subconscious memory. Not only does Ho'oponopono heal our relationship with ourselves, it also heals our relationships with others. To do this, simply visualise the person you want to heal from, place your hand over your heart and repeat the mantra 'Ho'oponopono' as many times as feels good.

Our words are incredibly powerful, with each one carrying a unique vibration. It is these vibrations that create much of the reality that surrounds us. This is something that has been taught throughout history; it is a consistent message throughout the Bible.

For example, God says, 'Let there be light' and as a result creates light. The Bible also states that the Universe was created through sound, 'In the beginning was the word, and the word was with God, and the word was God.'

One of my favourite sayings is 'your word is your wand'. I am always saying this to my children so that they understand the power of their words and how they can create through them. I had no idea about the law of attraction, vibration or the power of sound when I was growing up, so it's amazing to see them putting these tools into practice at such a young age. The younger generation needs spiritual tools more than ever to help counteract excessive screen time and social media addiction. The perfect antidote to this is getting outside and playing in nature. The frequency of the Earth will detox the energy field and reduce the effects of screen radiation. Mother Earth has a cure for pretty much everything and when it comes to raising your vibration she presents many pathways to support our conscious evolution.

Gaia

The Earth is a conscious intelligent life form; she breathes, feels, reacts; she is ever-evolving and it is essential that we humans evolve with her. Our disconnection to the Earth has massively impacted our health on every level.

The Earth is alive; her heartbeat supports and sustains our very existence.

This continuous pulsating electromagnetic frequency that is the Earth's heartbeat is scientifically know as 'the Schumann resonance'. Vibrating at 7.83 Hertz, it is otherwise known as 'the OM frequency'.

The Schumann Resonance is vital for human health and wellbeing, so much so that NASA now install their spaceships with this frequency to support their astronauts whilst in space.

The Earth's resonant frequency translates to an alpha/theta brainwave, which induces a relaxed and blissful dreamlike state. It is on this particular brainwave that cell regeneration and healing happens. Benefits like enhanced memory, stress reduction, grounding, clear thinking and overall rejuvenation of the body, mind and spirit are all equated to attuning to the Earth's natural resonant frequency.

There are many ways in which we can connect to and honour Gaia, in our everyday lives and through this consistent connection we can raise our vibration considerably. Here are a few examples of how we can do this:

Crystals

One of my favourite ways to connect with Gaia is through crystals, with each and every one being a creation from Gaia herself. Next time you pick up a crystal, take a moment to really study it. See the light that is locked inside it; there are often rainbow infractions encapsulated within. The shape, texture, colour and patterns within a crystal are truly remarkable.

Often there will be striations across the surface of quartz or amethyst crystals; the ancients believed these markings contained codes of wisdom from Gaia. If you find a crystal with such striations, try sitting quietly and tuning into it through meditation. Before you start, you can say a simple invocation such as this:

> *'I would like to connect to the energy and information within this crystal, raising my vibration and my conscious awareness. Thank you.'*

I have always been obsessed with crystals and as I walked my spiritual path I felt called to study them in more depth, so in 2015 I enrolled on a crystal healing course and became a certified crystal healer. I learned so many fascinating things about these amazing little gems (excuse the pun) and how we can use them to expand our consciousness and enhance our connection to the celestial realms. Crystals compliment pretty much all spiritual practices and are a great tool for aiding communication with the angels. Something like clear quartz is a great all-rounder as it amplifies the energy around it. Therefore, intention-setting and visualisation can be empowered through the use of quartz crystal. In fact, pretty much all the aforementioned vibe-lifting exercises can be empowered by quartz.

When using crystals to connect with the Archangels, I recommend the following:

- Raphael: Emerald, Green Aventurine, Jade

- Michael: Lapis Lazuli, Clear Quartz, Selenite

- Zadkiel: Amethyst, Purple Fluorite

- Uriel: Ruby, Pyrite, Tiger's Eye

- Gabriel: Clear Quartz, Diamond, Sunstone

- Ariel: Rose Quartz, Pink Tourmaline

- Haniel: Aqua Aura Quartz, Moonstone

- Jophiel: Citrine, Gold

Crystals are so much more than inanimate objects; they actually hold consciousness. The inventor and engineer Nikola Tesla famously said, 'In a crystal we have clear evidence of the existence of a formative life principle, and though we cannot understand the life of a crystal, it is nonetheless a living being.'

The ancients used crystals for all kinds of things, from storing huge amounts of data, to healing certain imbalances within the body. Science is only just beginning to understand the benefits of crystals and how they can aid us in modern-day life ... something the ancients knew intuitively.

Whenever I conduct Reiki sessions, I pretty much always use crystals to balance the chakras. By the end of the session, the client's chakras will have attuned to the energy field of the crystal, bringing it back into a state of alignment. We humans are very susceptible to energy; we attune to the vibrations that are around us, but crystals have a consistent energy field which is why they are so beneficial to have in the home and on the body. Our energy entrains to the coherent vibration of the crystals.

The following crystals will help to balance your chakras. Simply lie down and lay them in the centre of the chakras and relax to some calming music.

- **Crown:** Amethyst

- **Third eye:** Lapis Lazuli

- **Throat:** Blue Angelite

- **Heart:** Rose Quartz

- **Solar Plexus:** Citrine

- **Sacral:** Carnelian

- **Root:** Red Jasper

Some crystals can help to protect us against electromagnetic radiation (EMR) from our cellphones and WiFi etc. The general rule of thumb is the higher the iron content, the more protective against EMR. So, crystals like hematite, shungite, black tourmaline and pyrite are good choices.

Another great way to integrate crystal energy is through drinking crystal elixirs. Simply place a rose quartz in your water and allow its energy to infuse into it overnight. You can remove the crystal before drinking the water or, alternatively, you could invest in a crystal water bottle.

Water is another potent form of medicine from Gaia that can raise your vibe beyond measure!

The Wonder of Water

Water is massively under-valued and so few people realise its potential to heal and uplift. Not only is it a conductor of light, but it is also a conscious, intelligent life form that records the vibrations it is exposed to.

Our bodies are made up of around 70 per cent water, so our thoughts and feelings directly affect the water and flow of energy within our bodies, due to its easily programmable nature.

The Japanese scientist Masaru Emoto carried out many fascinating experiments with water by taking photographs of frozen crystals. The water was photographed before it was frozen, and then subjected to different words and intentions, before being photographed again. The difference between the before and after images are astounding.

Emoto discovered that when subjected to positive intentions, the water formed beautiful crystals and when subjected to negative intentions no crystals formed, leaving a disorderly void.

In his best-selling book, 'The Hidden Messages in Water,' he explains: 'Water has the ability to copy and memorise information' and to 'understand water is to understand the Cosmos, the marvels of nature, and life itself.'

It is important to note the experiments had to be done with natural water as tap water failed to create crystals due to the chemicals within it … hardly surprising, given the toxic waste added into our water systems.

Emoto experimented with different types of music and imagery. No matter what form of energy was exposed to the water, whether it be a photograph, the written word or sound, the water always responded to the vibration accordingly. Emoto said: 'Learning about water is like an exploration to discover how the Cosmos works, and the crystals revealed through water are like the portal into another dimension.'

Water ritual

1. Begin to experiment with your water in different ways and see how it makes you feel. Start by placing a label over your drinking water and write a positive word upon the label. This can be something such as LOVE, GRATITUDE, HEALING etc.

    If you are ever feeling unwell, label your water and as you drink it believe that the water is healing you. You can also program the water with healing intentions before drinking it, simply hold your hands over it and visualise healing energy flowing into the water. Alternatively, infuse the water with crystal energy, something like amethyst or green aventurine are great choices for healing.

The water will record the vibration of the healing crystal and therefore when you drink the water you will receive healing!

2. Reprogram the water within your body. Remember you are 70 per cent water, therefore you are highly programmable! Most of us allow ourselves to be programmed by external energies, but we can consciously start to reprogram ourselves and the cells within our bodies through self-love and mindfulness.

   Find an area of imbalance within your body and set your intention to reprogram that area and bring it into balance. Visualise the area healing and being brought into alignment as new healthy cells are formed within your body.

3. When you drink your water, be mindful of the journey that the water has taken to get to this point. Imagine how it has flowed from the highest of mountains, down ancient waterfalls, filtering through rocks and minerals, and now it is about to flow through you. Think of the beautiful earthy vibrations and nourishment you will receive from the water as you drink it and give gratitude to Gaia.

Mindful Eating

So many of us live the majority of our lives on autopilot, not taking a minute for ourselves to sit and enjoy our food. As a mum I am definitely guilty of rushing through mealtimes, or even worse skipping a meal altogether and eating the kids scraps instead ...not my finest hour!

Recently I began doing a specific type of fasting called Ekadashi, which is of the Hindu tradition. It honours the two major phases of the Moon – the New Moon and the Waxing Moon – and fasting is observed on the 11th day (Ekadashi means 'eleventh') of the lunar cycle.

I had never tried fasting in this way before, but felt a pull to do it. After just a few months of observing Ekadashi, my relationship with food began to change. After a 24-hour fast day, I would think so carefully about my first meal and I noticed no matter what was on my plate I would always gravitate towards the highest-vibrational foods first. It was like I was tuned in on a higher level to the energy of the food. I started to look at food completely differently, really taking my time to enjoy every mouthful. As I did this spiritual cleansing practice, I no longer wanted anything processed and my sugar craving began to wane. I would find myself snacking on rocket leaves and apples as opposed to crisps and biscuits. I never consciously chose to become a mindful eater and, don't get me wrong, there are times when I'm constantly on the go with the children and I'll eat a quick banana while driving the car, but on the whole I am much more mindful of food, what is in it and where it came from. If it's fresh, organic and from the earth it's a winner, if it's low-vibe processed junk, with more than five ingredients, it's gotta go! I cannot tell you how good I feel since becoming a more mindful eater. I genuinely enjoy my food and am so grateful to the earth for constantly providing for us.

Next time you eat something grown from the earth, take a closer look at the food and see the beauty within it. Have you ever really looked at the centre of an orange or a lemon? The sacred geometry that lies within the fruits of the earth is truly miraculous. Everything grown directly from Mother Earth contains light codes from the Sun, which is then absorbed into your body. You can raise your vibration considerably by eating plant-based foods direct from the earth. It is no coincidence that yogis and Buddhists are mostly vegan! Next time you go to eat a piece of fruit or a vegetable, take a moment to think of the light energy within it and be sure to thank Gaia and the abundant earth for always providing for you.

Tree Hugging

The tree-hugging hippies were definitely onto something. Trees are magical sentient organisms with their own intelligence. Did you know that the trees communicate with each other? When one tree is sick the other trees send healing to it via a complex underground fungal network called mycelium, pretty cool huh? They also communicate with each other through the ethers, via pheromones and scent signals.

Recent studies by the Leipzig University in Germany found that 'When a deer is biting a branch, the tree brings defending chemicals to make the leaves taste bad, yet when a human breaks the branch with his hands, the tree knows the difference, and brings in substances to heal the wound.'

My point is that trees are so much more intelligent than we can ever imagine and we should be conscious of our symbiotic relationship with them. What we breathe in, they breathe out and what they breathe in, we breathe out. If we look at the cross-section of a tree trunk, we can see a mirror of our fingerprints. If we look at the network of branches and twigs, it mirrors the bronchi and bronchioles within our very lungs.

If we look at the veins within a leaf, it mirrors the fine veins on the palms of our hands. Once we realise our incredible connection to the trees, we begin to connect to higher levels of awareness. Some of my most profound channellings have been through connecting to trees.

Recently, I went on a walk to some ancient woods in a beautiful English village called Burton. As always, I took time to connect to the trees, placing my hands upon the bark and giving gratitude. This is an instant vibe lifter and shifter; the vibration of gratitude with the vibration of nature is a double whammy! I decided to close my eyes and tune into the energy of the tree, asking for any messages to come through.

My main channels of communication (see page 23) are Clairvoyance and Claircognizance. I was shown streams of light flowing beneath my feet going down into the village. Ley lines, I thought, powerful ley lines are flowing through these woods. With my hands still connected to the tree, the messages began to flow into my mind with ease.

> *'This village carries the ancient codes from lands long ago when the divine feminine was honoured greatly. This energy is awakening and this ley line is becoming very active. Come to these woods often to recharge and receive higher guidance, it is a direct line to the divine.'*

As I came out of this channelling, I looked around to see where my husband was … he is very used to me having full on telepathic conversations with trees and tends to just leave me to it. Ha!

As I caught up with him and our dog Darla, I was going to tell him about the information I had received but then I got distracted and after a while the urge to share my experience with him had passed. 'He must be fed up of your strange ramblings,' I thought, 'keep it to yourself.' This was indeed my ego talking. As we left the woods and entered a little country lane, a message came through loud and clear to tell him about the download I had received. I know not to ignore my guides when they come through unexpectedly like that so out it came …

'Yeh, that was an amazing channelling with the tree back there.'

'Yeah?' he said.

'Yeh, I saw all of this powerful energy like a river of light flowing beneath the woods and then I was told it was ley lines. There's some powerful energy here that's really ancient yet still very active within the land.'

'Wow,' he said, 'pretty cool stuff, eh?'

'Yep' I said, 'sounds mad I know but I just felt the need to tell you.'

I always feel the need to say 'sounds crazy, or sounds mad' after one of my intuitive ramblings. It's a way of me letting my audience know that I'm well aware of how this sounds to the logical mind, but on the other hand I am super-tapped into my intuitive self, so it's not weird at all for me; it is totally my normal. I am grateful to have a husband that totally gets that about me. He has witnessed enough over the years to know that my intuition is a superpower and it shouldn't be doubted.

A few days later I was working from home with my bestie Nat who also happens to be my fabulous celestial assistant. She creates my epic monthly newsletters and we were brainstorming the theme for the latest one. We had been working non-stop while our kids played and entertained each other, but I was starting to get brain fog after too much screen time. 'Let's get outside in the garden,' I said to Nat.

'Great idea!' she said.

We put on our coats and bundled up the kids before heading out into the fresh winter air. As we strolled around the garden, I had an urge to go to a little ancient well nearby. It was the same feeling that I had received when I told my husband about the messages in the woods. 'Don't ignore it,' I thought.

'There is a gorgeous little well not far from here. I think we should venture out into the lanes and go see it. The kids will love it.'

'Okay, let's do it!' said Nat.

We arrived at the well and there were several members of the community digging away as part of a restoration project. A lady called Barbara came over and introduced herself, before proceeding to give us all an amazing history lesson on the magical Hampston's well.

We were fascinated by her knowledge of the area and I told her that you could really feel the magical energy of the whole village, especially at the woods.

'Oh, yes,' she said, 'well you know we found an ancient map of Burton not so long ago and on there it showed the powerful ancient energy lines that flow through Burton woods and out across the sea into Ireland.' I gasped with utter excitement at the very words that were flowing from her mouth.

'Wow, this is incredible. I was only at the woods two days ago and the same information came through! It felt like there was a very ancient divine feminine energy ley line that was active in the land.'

'Yes!' Barbara said, 'that's exactly what Emlyn said too. Emlyn is a local Druid who comes and honours the sacred water of the well. He's very tuned in.'

Wow, I mean you just can't make this stuff up. I was so excited to tell Barry about how this divine synchronicity had unfolded. It was another important reminder to continue to speak my truth, no matter how 'mad' it may sound to the logical mind. Bravery is always rewarded and if I had listened to my ego and not told Barry about the information I had received, then this story would not have held as much power. But as I had listened to the message to tell him, I had cemented the information into the physical and enabled a powerful communication to come through for others to hear also.

Nat was astonished. We walked back from the well buzzing about what had just played out and Nat had decided that the well would be the perfect feature for our monthly newsletter!

Tree Portal of Abundance & Awakening: This is one of my artworks inspired by the magic of trees and their ability to awaken us as we transcend into higher states of consciousness through connecting to them. The spiralling sacred geometry in the centre is a symbol of awakening.

Earthing

Earthing is another great way to lift your vibe and neutralise free radicals within the body. The practice of walking barefoot upon the earth has many benefits, such as helping to alleviate inflammation, insomnia, arthritis and depression. But how can something so simple be so effective?

Well, from a scientific angle we are electrical beings and when something with an electrical charge is connected to the ground its electric potential neutralises. The earth offers an abundant supply of free electrons, which help neutralise free radicals. Grounding to the earth in this way creates a natural flow between the earth and the body. Recent studies on earthing show that it can even alleviate chronic pain. It's time to take our shoes off and go outside!

Grounding is another great way to align your energy. Often when we connect regularly to the higher realms, we can feel a little ungrounded. After every healing session, I ground myself and my client as it helps them to integrate the light and wisdom received during the session. Even when conducting private online sessions with my clients, I always ground before and after. Whether connecting in person or across the ethers, it is equally as powerful and there is always so much light and higher guidance that flows through.

Grounding Ritual

You can do this grounding exercise anywhere. Whether inside your home or out in nature, grounding is super-quick and easy and can be done through a simple visualisation.

- Sit in a chair, placing both feet on the ground.

- Take a deep breath and imagine roots of light growing out of your feet burrowing deep into the earth.

- Visualise them moving down through the various layers the earth and anchoring to the centre of the earth's core.

- You are now grounded and rooted to the earth.

- You can also do this exercise standing.

Yoga

Any form of exercise is an instant vibe lifter and shifter but yoga is my daily go to for stretching, toning and strengthening my body, mind and spirit. I used to take yoga classes at my local studio in LA and Vinyassa Flow was always my favourite style as it is meditative and calming, yet you still get to work up a good sweat. However, in 2021 I initiated into the yogic practice of Surya Kriya with the Isha Foundation, founded by Sadhguru. 'Surya' means 'sun' and 'kriya' means 'inner energy process'. This potent practice activates the solar plexus chakra and balances the masculine and feminine energy channels within the body.

Practising this amazing technique every morning followed by meditation has been transformational. My day always begins with a solid foundation and I know that I am physically, mentally and spiritually strong as I navigate daily life.

As a busy mum I used to tell myself I did not have time to do yoga every day, but everything is a choice. I now choose to make time every day to take care of myself physically, mentally and spiritually. The great thing about yoga is that you can tick all these boxes in one 30-minute session and through aligning my energy in this way I actually create more time in my day!

I urge everyone to try yoga and feel the bliss of nurturing your body, mind and spirit. For more information on this kind of yoga, head to **isha.sadhguru.org**

Breathe

The breath is life! Most of us breathe at a fraction of the capacity we should, there are so many benefits to breathing deeply. Make it your mission to be more conscious of your breath. Breathing deeply opens the heart and the mind, something that the angels are constantly reminding us to do!

I highly recommend experimenting with breath work. The Wim Hof Method is a great place to start. Wim Hof has been making waves across the globe with his powerful take on breathwork. Just one session of breathwork alkalises the blood, boosting your immune system considerably. The benefits of oxygenating the body are remarkable, bringing immediate stress reduction, upliftment and mental clarity, to name just a few.

Personally, breathwork has been a key player in aiding my communication with the higher realms. Just three rounds of the Wim Hof Method puts me into such a deep state of relaxation that I am able to detach from the physical and travel into the void. Here I am in a state of complete alignment, and from this place I can hear the messages from spirit with clarity. Often I am taken on a journey, travelling to other worlds and dimensions – it's mind-blowing!

Sunshine and Starlight

We cannot live without the Sun; it is absolutely vital to our wellbeing.

In the words of the Indian guru, Sadhguru, 'If for 18 hours the sun disappeared, everything would cease to exist on the planet.' Now there is perspective right there.

It is so important to connect to the natural rhythms of the Earth. To gain the most benefit, connect with the light of the sunrise and soak up the rays of the sunset. This helps the body to be in flow with nature and its circadian rhythms.

There are huge benefits to stepping outside and getting a daily dose of sunlight and starlight. Did you know that getting the right balance of both can lift your mood and support your overall health considerably? Sunlight and starlight trigger the release of hormones in the brain. Sunlight releases the happy hormone known as serotonin, and starlight creates melatonin, making you feel all calm and dreamy, prepping you for a good night's sleep.

Soaking up the energy of the stars is pure magic. I love stepping out under a blanket of stars and contemplating the vastness of the Universe. Sometimes our celestial star friends will appear under a clear night sky, especially if you have an open heart and invite them in. I have seen many unusual hovering lights in the sky, which disappear in an instant. If you want to learn more about star beings, I highly recommend looking into the work of Dr Steven Greer, his work in this field is exemplary. The documentary 'Close Encounters of the Fifth Kind' is a fascinating watch and one that I highly recommend. It will blow your mind … in a good way.

Happy star gazing!

Spinning

Everything spins, from the smallest cell to the stars, planets and galaxies. Everything takes part in this perpetual revolving dance. The fundamental condition of our existence is to revolve.

I have a fun story to share. I have always loved spinning … and I'm talking spinning around and around like a spinning top, not the gruelling spinning that you would find at the likes of Soul Cycle. I've done that once and walked like a penguin for a week – it was not fun!

As a child, I would constantly spin for fun and it didn't stop at childhood. As a teenager, I continued with my spontaneous spinning. My mum would walk into the room to find me twirling like a mini tornado – she has long called me 'the whirling dervish' for this reason!

Even into my 20s and now 30s, I have continued to spin. I love the feeling that I get when I do it – it totally re-energises me and revives my inner child.

One day after a deep Wim Hof breathwork session, I was taken on a journey into another realm and I could see lots of spinning lights. As I focused in closer, I realised that these were actually light beings that were spinning. I asked telepathically why they were doing this and was told that they were rebooting their energy systems and aligning themselves. I couldn't believe that I had been spinning my whole life and never knew that there was a deeper meaning to it. This then prompted me to do a little more research into my fellow whirling dervishes and what I found out was fascinating. The ritual whirling of the dervishes presents an act of love and faith, with the dervishes seeking a state of transcendence. It is a mesmerizing display, inducing an ecstatic feeling of soaring and mystical flight. I discovered that Rumi and his followers also love a spinning ritual, integrating music into the practice – double whammy! In the words of Rumi:

> *'We come spinning out of nothingness,*
> *scattering stars like dust.'*

Okay, so I know spinning isn't everyone's cup of tea and you have to be pretty agile to do it, but if you are physically able, I highly recommend it – it's so much fun and instantly lifts your vibration. If you do decide to give spinning a try, please be careful and be sure to choose an open safe space to spin. I cannot be held responsible for any bumps or bruises incurred through spinning! Enjoy!

CHAPTER 14

RAISING THE VIBE OF THE ENTIRE PLANET

Sometimes it seems like there is so much darkness and hatred on the planet that we wonder how we can make a difference in this world. Back in the day when I used to watch the news, I often used to have a feeling of hopelessness. I would be in floods of tears after watching reports of the atrocities happening around the world and it would take me days to shake off that heavy energy.

However, once I began to walk my spiritual path and awaken to the power of my own personal vibration, I realised that my feelings of despair and hopelessness were helping no one; in fact, they were only adding to the problem because individual consciousness affects the collective consciousness.

We are each branches of the same tree, we are conscious beings connected to a complex web of energy that creates the collective experience. If the mass consciousness is dominated by fear then fearful experiences become dominant on the planet.

So through watching the devastating global events on the news and spiralling into hopelessness and despair, I am only adding that energy to the collective and therefore creating more fear.

If there is one thing you take away from this book let it be the knowing that you are a powerful being and you can make a difference, a huge difference. Change starts with you. Do not worry about trying to change anyone else. Shining your light and leading by example is the most powerful thing that you can do to help the planet. Be the light.

Now that I realise how powerful I am and that I really can make a difference to the world, I react differently to such events. Instead of allowing myself to wallow in sorrow and despair, I connect to the light. I call in all the angels and light beings to help my fellow humans who are in need, and I counteract the fear energy by sending love. Love is indeed our greatest weapon. When we open our hearts and act from a place of love, not only do we counteract the energy of fear, we also over ride it. In the words of Abraham Hicks;

> *'One person who is in alignment is more powerful than millions who are not.'*

Our thoughts are powerful projections to the Universe and when we come together with one unified vision, we can move mountains.

Have you ever heard of the 1 per cent effect? This theorises that 1 percent of conscious humans can transform the rest of the 99 percent. It has been consistently proven in consciousness studies and in the world of quantum mechanics.

There are many scientists and spiritual teachers that talk of the
1 percent effect which is also known as the Maharishi effect.

Yogi Maharishi Mahesh often spoke of this fascinating phenomenon in
relation to Transcendental Meditation and the global peace that would ensue
if as little as 1 percent of the world's population practised this powerful
meditation technique.

There have been hundreds of experiments conducted demonstrating the
power and efficacy of the 1 percent effect with Transcendental Meditation.
In 1975 scientific research was released with results showing significant
reductions in crime rates across 12 American cities when 1 percent of each
city's population practised the TM technique.

The following is an excerpt from the book 'Enlightenment Invincibility:
to Every Individual, to Every Nation' by Maharishi Mahesh Yogi;

> *'When the body becomes better, the mind becomes better,*
> *the behavior becomes better. With this orderly brain, a*
> *few people—1 percent … can improve the trends of life.*
> *It requires only a few people, just a few people!'*

The practice of meditation creates order and coherence within the mind.
If we look at the Meissner Effect, we can begin to understand the science
behind why the 1 percent effect works. This is the scientifically proven
phenomena in which internally coherent systems have the ability to
repel external influences, and incoherent systems are easily penetrated
by disorder from the outside.

Simply put, if we are in a state of disorder/fear we are extremely programmable as we are easily penetrated by external energies of disorder … and boy are we bombarded with those! However, if we are in a state of order/alignment we repel the energy of disorder and further more we begin to penetrate the external energies of disorder. Through our aligned state we neutralise all those disorderly frequencies that create fear and dis-ease, so by taking responsibility for our mental health and balancing the mind every day through meditation, we are being of great service to the whole. Maharishi Mahesh Yogi describes this concept beautifully when he says;

> *'What is a bulb? It is a very small filament. How much is that in relation to the whole volume of the room? It's a very insignificant area. Yet it becomes lighted and the whole room becomes lighted. One simple, single individual brain becoming a little bit more orderly … One small filament becoming lighted is enough to light the whole room. Like that, one person, one slightly enlightened person, is a blessing for the whole society.'*

You can be a blessing to society, you can be the filament in the light bulb radiating light across the room.

Do not underestimate the power that you hold and the healing ripple effect that you can have on those around you through your consistent connection to the light.

The very nature of life is to grow, yet most of us stunt our own growth as we get caught up in battles of the ego with all the distractions and dramas of the material world, never realising our souls true purpose or potential.

Your desire to grow and evolve is what has brought you to be here reading this book.

You are here to create change within yourself and that is enough.

As you connect to the celestial realms and awaken to the power of the Goddess, you will open yourself up to a whole new world of magic and miracles as you begin to walk your highest path of light.

You are part of the 1 percent that chose to be here on Earth at this time to create powerful change, and so am I ... there are more of us than you might think.

With the mass awakening that is happening right now, many lights are being switched on as we remember the multi-dimensional nature of our souls. Soon enough we will reach that 1 per cent and when we do there will be a tsunami of light across the planet; this will be the monumental shift to the fifth, this will be the New Earth.

Thank you, my fellow light warrior for taking on this mission and helping to bring in the dawn of a new Golden Age. Thank you for aligning to the light and igniting the sacred fire of your soul.

STAY CONNECTED

Newsletter

To stay connected with me and receive updates on any upcoming events, you can sign up to my monthly celestial newsletter. When you subscribe you will also receive one of my angelic meditations as a special gift.

www.katysloane.com/newsletter

Celestial Tribe Membership

A sacred online space where like minded souls can come together and connect with the angelic realms every week, bringing a constant flow of celestial light into your life.

Joining my tribe will help you to shift out of fear, bringing inner peace, love and joy. There are 3 different levels of membership to suit all.

www.katysloane.com/celestial-tribe

Courses

Archangelolology Level 1

Celestial Goddess Rising

Reiki level 1, level 2, Master level and Teacher level

www.katysloane.com/courses

The Ether Real Podcast

In this podcast we explore the very nature of reality; what is more real, the physical or the ethereal? Addressing real life issues, we discuss how to heal and align our energy through connecting to our celestial team and the unseen realms.

As more and more people turn to mindfulness and spiritual practices, it is time to bring the supernatural world of angels, guides and star beings to the collective mainstream.

www.katysloane.com/podcast

Art Gallery

All of my artwork is imbued with angelic and celestial frequencies. Head over to my website and browse my shop to explore connecting to the higher realms through art.

www.katysloane.com/shop

ACKNOWLEDGEMENTS

To Barry, my husband, my soul mate, my divine masculine counterpart. Thank you for being my rock and for supporting me in everything that I do. It is amazing to see how far we have come together on our journey. Our achievements are each others', our stories interwoven into one beautiful life canvas. Thank you. I love you.

To Gracie Blue, thank you for being my greatest teacher. You are the most beautiful soul inside and out and I am so proud of you. Keep shining your light, and never let anyone dull your sparkle. It is because of you that I am here writing this book. You corrected my course and set me on this path of light. Thank you. I love you.

To Lennon, my bestest buddy! Thank you for bringing so much joy into our lives. You light up the room, bringing fun and laughter wherever you go. What a blessing you are my sweetheart. I am so grateful you chose me to be your mummy. I love you to infinity and beyond.

To Mum and Dad, thank you for always being there and for having the children at the drop of a hat. Those spontaneous writers retreats played a huge part in helping me to complete this book. It would not have been possible without you stepping up to help with the children…those bunk beds sure came in handy! Thank you for everything!

To Sarah, my starseed sister and partner in crime. You are so much more than a sister to me; you are an earth angel, a wise white witch and a goddess from the stars. The things that we have witnessed and experienced together on our spiritual path has created a bond that is unbreakable. Thank you for choosing to live and continue your mission here on Earth. You are so gifted and give so much light to others. Thank you for being you!

Stanley, what a brave and special soul you are. You signed up for a big mission when you came to Earth. I am so inspired by your fighting spirit and forever grateful for the lessons and growth you have brought to us all. You are a hero little man and I couldn't be a prouder auntie.

To Michael, thank you for being the best big bro and for always making me laugh! Thank you for being the life and soul of the party, and for dressing up as teen wolf against your will… no one will ever beat that costume!

To Joy and Paul, thank you for the weekends of fun and laughter with the children and for giving me the freedom to write and have time to myself. I am so grateful!

To Nat, my bestie since the age of 3. Thank you for being a constant support for me and for always having my back. Who would ever have thought that we would join forces to become the celestial dream team that we are?!

You are the bestest friend and celestial assistant I could ever wish for - from your epic monthly newsletters, to the magical Celestial Tribe Membership you helped create. You keep everything ticking! Thank you for helping to bring this book into existence, I couldn't have done it without you!!!

To Liz, how far we have come since our student fashionista days! Our trip to San Diego was a turning point for me, you made me see that I was ready to step out on to the stage and share my truth. Thank you for being a part of the celestial dream team! I am so grateful for your talents and friendship.

To Camilla, thank you for your guidance and support. You have planted so many seeds of light on my path - from my first art exhibition to the creation of this book. I am so grateful for our friendship… you are one in a million.

To Sky, thank you for your friendship, knowledge and expertise. Your nuggets of wisdom have accelerated me along my spiritual path in divine ways. I am so grateful for you my dear friend.

To Calista, my angel sister. I am so grateful for your support. Thank you for introducing me to Sean at 'The Good House,' you knew we were the perfect match!

To Sean Patrick, thank you for the coffee's, the laughs and for being there to answer my constant flurry of questions. We make an awesome team my fellow thespian! I am so grateful to be a 'TGH' author. Thank you!

To Dawn Bates, thank you for all of your support with the editing process. I am so grateful for your presence, support and expertise.

To Faye, thank you for your incredible work - from the magical front cover, to the beautiful formatting. You have brought the pages to life and surpassed my expectations. Thank you!

To the Unplug community in Los Angeles, thank you for your phenomenal support over the years. Connecting with you all from this beautiful space lights me up and drives me to continue spreading this important message.

To my amazing clients, I am so grateful for our magical sessions. Getting to know you on a soul level is my honour. The signs, synchronicities and angelic wisdom we experience together never ceases to amaze me. As I play the role of teacher, I am aware that I am also the student. I learn so much from each and every one of you, thank you!

To my awesome Celestial Tribe members, thank you for your amazing support. You consistently show up to connect to the light and it is because of you that I get to host these magical classes. I am so blessed to have this uplifting community of beautiful souls.

And last but by no means least, thank you to my celestial team, the archangels, the Essenes, Yeshua, Mary Magdalene, and the Goddess Sophia; for awakening me to levels I could never have dreamed possible. May you continue to guide me on this path of light. Thank you!

BIBLIOGRAPHY

Byrne, Lorna (2010),
Angels in My Hair,
Arrow

Byrne, Rhonda (2006),
The Secret,
Simon & Schuster UK

Cannon, Dolores (1993),
Between Death and Life:
Conversations with a Spirit,
Ozark Mountain Publishing

Cannon, Dolores (2002),
Jesus and the Essenes,
Ozark Mountain Publishing

Cannon, Dolores (2011),
Three Waves of Volunteers
and the New Earth,
Ozark Mountain Publishing

Durek, Shaman (2020),
Spirit Hacking: Shamanic
keys to reclaim your personal
power, transform yourself and
light up the world,
Yellow Kite

Emoto, Masaru (2005),
Hidden Messages in Water,
Pocket Books

Foor, Daniel (2017),
Ancestral Medicine: Rituals for
Personal and Family Healing,
Bear & Company

Hurtak, J.J (1996),
The book of knowledge:
The keys of Enoch,
The Academy for Future Science

Hurtak, J.J (1999),
Pistis Sophia: A Coptic Gnostic –
Text with Commentary,
Academy for Future Science

Jowett, George F. (2009),
Drama of the Lost Disciples,
Covenant Publishing Co Ltd

Lipton, Bruce (2010),
The Biology of Belief: Unleashing
The Power of Consciousness,
Matter & Miracles, Hay House

Mahesh Yogi, Maharishi (1986),
Enlightenment Invincibility: To
Every Individual, to Every Nation,
Agenda

McCannon, Tricia (2015),
Return of the Divine Sophia:
Healing the Earth through the Lost
Wisdom Teachings of Jesus, Isis,
and Mary Magdalene,
Bear & Company

Melchizedek, Drunvalo (1999),
The Ancient Secret of the
Flower of Life,
Light Technology US

Meurois-Givaudan,
Anne and Daniel (1993),
Way of the Essenes: Christ's Hidden
Life Remembered, Inner Traditions
Bear and Company

Muhl, Lars (2014),
The Law of Light:
The Secret Teachings of Jesus,
Watkins Publishing

Shumsky, Susan (2013),
The Power of Auras: Tap
Into Your Energy Field for Clarity,
Peace of Mind, and Well-Being,
New Page Books.

Watterson, Meggan (2021),
Mary Magdalene Revealed:
The First Apostle, Her Feminist
Gospel & the Christianity
We Haven't Tried Yet,
Hay House UK

Wohlleben, Peter, (2017)
The Hidden Life of Trees,
Harper Collins Publishers.

ARCHANGEL SUMMARY

At this point in your life's journey there will be specific archangels that will be working with you more closely than others. This all depends on where you are on your life path and what you need most. For example, if we are in need of deep healing Raphael will be close by, or if we are seeking more cosmic connection then Haniel will be there for us.

Review the list of archangels below and circle the ones that you feel most connected to at this point in your life:

Archangel Michael
Strength, protection,
releasing fears.
Colour: Electric blue

Archangel Raphael
Healing, loving relationships,
heart activation
Colour: Emerald green

Archangel Zadkiel

Violet flame, transmuting lower
energies, crown chakra balancing.
Colour: Violet

Archangel Ariel

Connection to Earth & animals,
grounding, manifesting abundance.
Colour: Pink

Archangel Uriel

Wisdom, lifting the veils
of illusion, truth.
Colour: Red, Gold

Archangel Haniel

Cosmic connection,
moon cycles, intuition.
Colour: Turquoise, Silver

Archangel Gabriel

Speaking your truth, receiving
messages, inner child.
Colour: White, Rose Gold, Copper

Archangel Jophiel

Beauty, artistic expression,
connection to Divine Mother.
Colour: Yellow, Gold

Angel Numbers and Meanings

1111: Angels are guiding you and reminding you of their presence.

222: The archangels are supporting and empowering you in all that you do.

333: You are shifting into a higher consciousness – keep connecting to Source.

444: The great ascended masters are watching over you.

555: A time of huge positive changes.

CPSIA information can be obtained
at www.ICGtesting.com
Printed in the USA
LVHW010036181122
733281LV00011B/623